Aeschylus · I

ORESTEIA

THE COMPLETE GREEK TRAGEDIES

Edited by David Grene and Richmond Lattimore

Aeschylus · I

ORESTEIA

AGAMEMNON

THE LIBATION BEARERS

THE EUMENIDES

Translated
and with an Introduction by
RICHMOND LATTIMORE

THE UNIVERSITY OF CHICAGO PRESS

CHICAGO & LONDON

THE UNIVERSITY OF CHICAGO PRESS, CHICAGO & LONDON
The University of Toronto Press, Toronto 5, Canada

Copyright 1953 by The University of Chicago. All rights reserved Copyright 1953 under the International Copyright Union. Published 1953. Thirteenth Impression 1964. Composed and printed by THE UNIVERSITY OF CHICAGO PRESS, *Chicago, Illinois, U.S.A.*

NOTE

The translation of *Agamemnon* which is here used first appeared in *Greek Plays in Modern Translation*, edited with an Introduction by Dudley Fitts (New York: Dial Press, 1947). It is used here by kind permission of The Dial Press, Inc. Some alterations have been made, chiefly in the matter of spelling Greek names. Two sections of *Agamemnon*, "The God of War, Money Changer of Dead Bodies," and "The Achaeans Have Got Troy, upon This Very Day," first published in *War and the Poet: A Comprehensive Anthology of the World's Great War Poetry*, edited by Richard Eberhart and Selden Rodman, are used by permission of the Devin-Adair Company.

The translation of all three plays is based on H. W. Smyth's "Loeb Classical Library" text (London and New York: William Heinemann, Ltd., and G. P. Putnam's Sons, 1926). A few deviations from this text occur where I have followed the manuscript readings instead of emendations accepted by Smyth.

Various editions of Greek drama divide the lines of lyric passages in various ways, but editors regularly follow the traditional line numbers whether their own line divisions tally with these numbers or not. This accounts for what may appear to be erratic line numbering in our translations, for instance, *The Eumenides* 360 and following. The line numbering in the translations in this volume is that of Smyth's text.

TABLE OF CONTENTS

INTRODUCTION TO THE *ORESTEIA*

The Life of Aeschylus

Aᴇꜱᴄʜʏʟᴜꜱ, the son of Euphorion, was born in the last quarter of the sixth century B.C., probably about 513 or 512 B.C. The great Persian Wars occurred during his early manhood, and he fought, certainly at Marathon (where his brother was killed in action) and probably also at Artemisium, Salamis, and Plataea. He is said to have begun at an early age to write tragedies; his first victory was in 484 B.C. In or about 476 B.C. he visited Sicily and, at the instance of Hieron of Syracuse, Pindar's friend, produced *The Women of Etna* at the new city of Etna which Hieron had founded. In 472 he produced his *Persians* at Athens, with Pericles as his choregus (or official sponsor) and re-produced it, presumably in the next year, in Sicily. Back in Athens in 468, he was defeated by the young Sophocles, but won again in 467 with a set of plays including *The Seven against Thebes*. In 458 he presented the *Oresteia* (*Agamemnon, The Libation Bearers, The Eumenides*). He died in Gela, Sicily, in 456 or 455 B.C., leaving behind him an epitaph which might be rendered as follows:

Under this monument lies Aeschylus the Athenian,
    Euphorion's son, who died in the wheatlands of Gela. The grove
of Marathon with its glories can speak of his valor in battle.
    The long-haired Persian remembers and can speak of it too.

He left behind more than seventy plays (the exact number is uncertain), of which seven have survived. They are *The Suppliants, The Persians, The Seven against Thebes, Prometheus Bound, Agamemnon, The Libation Bearers, The Eumenides.* He is said to have won first prize thirteen times while he lived, but after his death his tragedies were often produced again, and in competition with living poets he won more prizes still.

It would be interesting to know how old Aeschylus was when he wrote his known and dated plays. But the date of his birth is quite uncertain, though the year 525/4[1] is commonly given as if it were an established fact. It is true enough that apparently independent authorities give ages at the time of Marathon and at time of death which agree with this scheme. However, the birth date may very easily be accounted for by the rule-of-thumb method, favored by Greek chronologists, of taking an important event in a man's life and counting back forty years to an estimated date of birth. Thus the traditional birth date of Thucydides is 471 (from the outbreak of the war he recorded in 431); of Aristophanes, 445 (from the production of his masterpiece, *The Frogs*, in 405). Both these dates are bad (there are many parallels), and the one for Aeschylus is no more convincing. An age of forty at his first victory is suspect, not only because it tallies so neatly with a known method of reckoning, but because it is in itself unlikely that a man who utterly eclipsed his rivals in subsequent reputation, so that they are now very little more than bare names, should have had to wait so long before scoring his first success. A less popular but more attractive tradition would make him born in 513 or 512, but here also we may be dealing with estimates based on known and dated events, such as battles and dramatic productions.

Ancient authorities also tell us a few other things about Aeschylus which would be interesting if we could believe them. It is said that he left Athens for Sicily in chagrin because he was defeated by Simonides, the great lyric poet, in a competition for writing the epitaph of the dead at Marathon, or because he was defeated by Sophocles in dramatic competition, or because he disliked Athenian politics.[2]

1. Athenian dates are generally fixed by the term of the *archon*, or titular chief magistrate. Since the archons changed over some time in the summer, not at our new year, such dates overlap those of our calendar. Since, however, plays came out in the spring before the change-over, a play dated to an archonship of, for instance, 485/4 will *always* fall in 484.

2. Euripides, near the end of his life, left Athens in voluntary exile and died in Macedonia at the court of King Archelaus. There is reason to believe that he left because he had constantly failed to win critical approval in Athens and because he despaired of the hopeless course which his city had been following since the time of Pericles. The biographers doubtless applied the analogy of Euripides-Athens-Arche-

The defeats are real, but they do not tally, chronologically, with the visits to Sicily; on the contrary, after losing to Sophocles, Aeschylus stayed in Athens and won first prize with *The Seven against Thebes* and its related dramas the next year, which is quite different from going off to Sicily in a huff. If one may guess at why he went to Sicily, it was because Sicily was the America of that day, the new Greek world, rich, generous, and young, with its own artists but without the tradition of perfected culture which Old Greece had built up, and it attracted Pindar, Bacchylides, Simonides, and Aeschylus much as America has attracted English men of letters from Dickens, Thackeray, and Wilde down to the present day. We do not know much about the personal character of Aeschylus and can make little critical use of what we do know. The epitaph shows he was proud of his military record, but this scarcely helps us to understand *The Persians*, *The Seven against Thebes*, or *Agamemnon*. We must approach Aeschylus, not from the biographies, but from his own plays.

Early Tragedy

From the time of the almost legendary Thespis, a full generation before the earliest tragedy we possess, dramatic performances of some sort had been regularly produced at Athens. In origin, they must have been a special local development of the choral lyric—sacred, occasional, provincial, public—which was alive in all the cities of Greece. But the early phases of the course by which dramatic lyric was transformed into lyric drama are now invisible to us. We can recognize certain ingredients, or essential features. Early drama was choral, and the life of Attic tragedy shows the indispensable chorus to the end, though the actors steadily invade the preserves of the chorus until, at the close of the fifth century, Euripides is using it sometimes in a most perfunctory manner, as if it were a convention he could not get rid of but might otherwise have preferred to do without. Early drama was sacred, having to do with the

---

laus to Aeschylus-Athens-Hieron. But Euripides was a failure in his own lifetime, and it made him a defeatist and escapist. Of Aeschylus we can say with confidence that he was neither of these things.

cult of divinities, and particularly with the cult of Dionysus: on the formal side, it was performed to the end on ground devoted to that god and before his priest; but developed tragedy did not have to be *about* Dionysus, and seldom was. Like most choral lyric, it was given through the medium of a formal competition. The early tragic poets drew, for narrative material and for metrical forms, on an already rich and highly developed tradition of nondramatic poetry, epic and lyric. They also drew, no doubt, on the unwritten and almost inarticulate experience of a living people, on folk memory and folklore, cult and ritual and ceremony and passion play and mystery play. But tragedy did not grow out of such elements. It was made. Concerning the makers, we know little indeed about Thespis, Pratinas, Choerilus, Phrynichus. Tragedy, for us, begins with Aeschylus.

By or during the career of Aeschylus, the features of Greek tragedy become fixed. At an Athenian festival, three player-groups, each consisting of two (later three) actors and chorus, act out competitively four-drama sets. The material is based on stories told or indicated in previous Greek legend. Tragedy is heroic. The costumes are formal, physical action restrained and without violence; naturalism is neither achieved nor desired. Aeschylus himself, and his older contemporary Phrynichus before him, experimented with dramatic stories taken from contemporary history, and of these we have *The Persians*, dealing with the repulse of Xerxes and his forces. This was a success, but circumstances in this case were favorable to special occasional drama, for the defeat of Persia was the proudest achievement of Greek history. And, even here, the play is *about* the Persians, not the Greeks, the setting is Persia, and only Persian individuals are named. Remoteness from the immediate here-and-now, required by tragedy and guaranteed by legendary material, is here to a great extent achieved by placing the scene in the heart of Persia, so far away and guarded from Greeks that to the audience it might have seemed almost as legendary as the Troy of Hector or the Thebes of Oedipus.[3] A drama dealing directly with Themistocles and Pericles or

3. So Shakespeare drew on history and legend for his tragedies and romances, or, when these dealt with time not specifically antique, the place would be idealized by

with the war between Athens and Aegina would have been neither desired by the poet nor tolerated by his audience.

The body of legend on which Aeschylus and the other tragic poets drew was composed of the epic poems of Homer and his successors and constituted a loose and informal, but fairly comprehensive, history of the world as the Greeks knew it. Typical sources in this complex were the *Iliad* and the *Odyssey;* the "Epic Cycle," or series of subsequent epics which filled out the story of Troy and dealt in detail with its occasions and aftereffects; the epics that told the story of Thebes; and numerous other narratives either written down or transmitted through unwritten oral tradition. The dramatist rarely worked directly from the main body of the *Iliad* or the *Odyssey;* the less authoritative minor texts were more popular. The dramatist seems not to have felt free to invent his material outright, but he could—in fact, he must—choose among variants, expand or deepen and interpret character, generally shape the story on the trend of his own imagination. In the case of Aeschylus, this process can be best reconstructed in the *Oresteia,* the trilogy or sequence of three tragedies composed of *Agamemnon, The Libation Bearers,* and *The Eumenides.*

The Story of the House of Atreus

The version of the legend as Aeschylus used it runs as follows. Atreus and Thyestes, the sons of Pelops, quarreled because Thyestes had seduced his brother's wife, and disputed the throne of Argos. Thyestes, defeated and driven out, returned as a suppliant with his children, and Atreus in pretended reconciliation invited him and his children to a feast. There he slaughtered the children of Thyestes (all but one) and served them in a concealing dish to their father, who ate their flesh. When it was made known to him what he had been doing, Thyestes cursed the entire house and fled with his surviving son, Aegisthus. Agamemnon and Menelaus, the sons of Atreus, inherited the Kingdom of Argos, and married, respectively, Clytae-

---

distance and the vagueness of his audience's information: Italy, Bohemia, Illyria, Arden.

mestra and Helen, the daughters of Tyndareus the Spartan. Clytaemestra bore Agamemnon three children—Iphigeneia, Electra,
and Orestes. When Paris of Troy seduced Helen and carried her
away, the brothers organized a great expedition to win her back.
The armament, gathered at Aulis, was held there by wind and
weather; Calchas the prophet divined that this was due to the anger
of Artemis and, with the pressure of public opinion behind him,
forced Agamemnon to sacrifice his daughter, Iphigeneia, in order
to appease the goddess. Agamemnon with his forces sailed to Troy
and in the tenth year captured it, destroyed the city and its temples,
killed or enslaved the people, and set sail for home. On the sea, a
great storm struck the fleet, and Agamemnon, with a single galley,
made his way back to Argos, the rest of his ships being sunk or
driven out of sight and knowledge. With him he brought his mistress, Cassandra, captive princess and prophetess of Troy.

Meanwhile, in Argos, Aegisthus had returned and Clytaemestra
had taken him as her lover and sent Orestes out of the country.
Warned of the king's approach by signal flares through which he
had agreed to notify her of the fall of Troy, she made ready to receive him. She welcomed him into the house, but when he was un-
armed in his bath, she pinioned him in a robe and stabbed him to
death, and killed Cassandra as well. She defended her action before
the people of Argos, who were helpless against Aegisthus and his
bodyguard. But Orestes returned at last and was welcomed by his
sister Electra, who had remained rebellious against her mother but
without power to act. Orestes, disguised as a traveler and pretending
to bring news of his own death, won access to the house and killed
both Aegisthus and Clytaemestra. Portents and dreams had fore-
warned of this murder, and Orestes had been encouraged, even commanded, by Apollo to carry it through. Nevertheless, when he had
displayed the bodies and defended his act, the Furies (Eumenides),
or spirits of retribution, appeared to him and drove him out of Argos. Orestes took refuge with Apollo at Delphi and was at last
purified of the murder, but the Furies refused to acknowledge any
absolution and pursued him across the world until he took refuge on
the rock of Athens before the statue of Athene. There, in the pres-

ence of Athene, Apollo and the Furies appealed to her for a decision, and she, thinking the case too difficult to be judged by a single person, even her divine self, appointed a court of Athenian jurors to hear the arguments and judge the case. When the votes of these resulted in a tie, Athene herself cast the deciding ballot in favor of Orestes. Orestes, deeply grateful to Athene and her city, returned to Argos, while Athene found it necessary to propitiate the angry Eumenides by inducing them to accept an honorable place as tutelary spirits in Athens. The law court of the Areiopagus, which had judged the case, was perpetuated as a just tribunal for homicide down through the history of man.

Variations of the Legend

Such are the bare facts of the story, the raw stuff out of which Aeschylus forged three massive tragedies. The story of the murder of Agamemnon had been told by Homer in the *Odyssey*[4] and by the cyclic successors of Homer in the *Nostoi* ("Returns"), while the early part of the story appears in the *Cypria*. Stesichorus, the Sicilian poet, had made the fortunes of Orestes the subject of a long narrative in lyric form; and Pindar in his *Eleventh Pythian* had summarized the tale and reflected on the motives of Clytaemestra; and others, too, had touched on the story. On all these Aeschylus doubtless drew, and he had numerous variations from which to pick and choose.[5] The main difference between Aeschylus and Homer is to be found, however, not in details but in the whole approach to the

4. Piecemeal: the plot is constantly referred to by analogy with the plot of the *Odyssey*. The principal references are: i. 29–43, Zeus calls the vengeance of Orestes an example of just retribution; i. 298–300, Athene uses it as an encouragement to Telemachus; iii. 254–312, Nestor tells Telemachus of the beguiling of Clytaemestra, the wanderings of Menelaus, and the vengeance of Orestes; iv. 514–37, Menelaus tells how he heard from Proteus about the death of Agamemnon; xi. 405–34, the ghost of Agamemnon tells Odysseus how his wife and Aegisthus murdered him and Cassandra.

5. For example, Homer makes the scene of the murder (and consequently the palace of Agamemnon) Mycenae; Stesichorus and Simonides, Sparta; Pindar, Amyclae (which comes to the same thing); Aeschylus, Argos, doubtless for political reasons. Stesichorus called the nurse of Orestes Laodameia; Pindar, Arsinoë; Aeschylus, Cilissa; etc.

story, which, in turn, motivates selection, addition, or omission of detail. It is to be noted that Homer does not tell the story consecutively; he really does not tell it at all, but he draws on it for example and illustration. The homecoming of Agamemnon is played against the homecoming of Odysseus; the situations are analogous, but the characters are different and bring different results out of similar materials. The murderous suitors lurk in the house of Odysseus as did Aegisthus in that of Agamemnon, but Penelope has not joined the enemy as Clytaemestra did. Nevertheless, when Odysseus comes home, he has his warning from the ghost of Agamemnon and goes warily so as not to fall into a similar trap. As for Telemachus, the resolute activity of Orestes is set as an example against his own indecision. The parts of the story that bear on such an apposition come out, and the tendency of it varies accordingly. The story is a domestic tragedy, but, since the house is a king's house, the tragedy becomes dynastic also. It begins with the betrayal of a king and the alienation of his kingdom and ends with the rewinning of dynastic power by the rightful heir. Therefore, though the death of Agamemnon is tragic, the deaths of Aegisthus and Clytaemestra are nothing of the sort; no tragedy adheres to Orestes, he merits no compassion, only praise. It is, I think, because of this *approach* that Homer fails to mention certain aspects of the story which are prominent in Attic tragedy. Iphigeneia does not appear; her slaughter would have suggested some motive of justice mixed into the treachery of Clytaemestra. Nor do we hear of the wrongs inflicted by Atreus on Thyestes and his sons, for this would have made the murder of Agamemnon in some measure defensible as an act of retribution. Nowhere in Homer do we hear of an Orestes pursued by the Furies of his mother, whether these might be actual spirits or the remorse in his own memory. Did Homer, then, know nothing of how Orestes murdered Clytaemestra? The lines in which he speaks of her death betray him (*Od.* iii. 304–10), for, while Menelaus was still on his travels,

> Seven years Aegisthus was lord in golden Mycenae,
> but in the eighth the evil came on him when great Orestes
> came back from Athens and killed his father's slayer, the crafty

Aegisthus, who had murdered his glorious father. And after
he had killed him, in the Argives' presence he held a funeral
for his mother, who was hateful, and for the coward Aegisthus.

This unobtrusive notice is all we have, but it makes perfectly plain
the fact that the matricide was in Homer's tradition, and he could
not contradict it. But he was in a position to place the emphasis
wherever he chose and to tell only as much of the story, or as little,
as suited his purpose. It is surely no accident that the parts which he
leaves out are those which would complicate and confuse his simple
picture of Aegisthus as a conspiring villain, Orestes as an avenging
hero, and Clytaemestra as a woman who yielded to her weakness.

Aeschylus, on the other hand, told the whole story. *Agamemnon* takes us from the news of Troy's fall to the murder of Agamemnon and the confirmation of his murderers as despots in Argos. *The Libation Bearers* begins with the return of Orestes and ends with his flight from Argos, pursued by the Furies, after the murder of Clytaemestra and Aegisthus. *The Eumenides* finds Orestes seeking sanctuary at Delphi, takes him to Athens for his acquittal and absolution, and ends with the establishment of the Furies in their new home at Athens. Further, particularly in the first play of the trilogy, there are constant cutbacks which sweep into the drama much of the foregoing material: the banquet of Thyestes, the sacrifice of Iphigeneia, the siege and fall of Troy. The simple narrative which we can reconstruct from notices in Homer could not have carried the weight of a tragic trilogy.

"Agamemnon"

Agamemnon is, first of all, a domestic tragedy. The dominant figure, Clytaemestra, is a wife estranged through the wrong her husband committed on their daughter; love for Iphigeneia, acting through the murder of Agamemnon, is on its way toward driving her to fight her love for her surviving daughter and for her son. Her paramour and partner is her husband's cousin. Behind them all is the figure of Helen, Clytaemestra's sister, wife of Agamemnon's brother, whose treachery caused the Trojan War, Iphigeneia's death, and all the estrangement and broken faith that followed. The theme here is the *philos-aphilos* or hate-in-love; its drive is the dynamic force of contradiction.

Behind the domestic tragedy lies the tragedy of war. For the sake of Helen, whose beauty was unforgettable but whose worth could not be demonstrated by reason or defended by argument, Agamemnon drained Greece of its manhood and involved the innocent in the miseries of a bitter campaign. The Trojans welcomed Helen and her captor and so were guilty; but their punishment—the total destruction of their city, their temples, and their men; the enslavement and defiling of their women and children—was out of all proportion to any harm they had done to Greece. Neither Troy nor Greece deserved what the idea of Helen made Agamemnon do to them. For he destroyed his own country as well as Troy; many died in the years before Ilium, the survivors were drowned or scattered in the great storm on the way back; and the pomp of his entrance thinly disguises the fact that he brought home the crew of a single ship.

Because of this, with the war tragedy goes political tragedy as well. The means by which this is communicated is through the chorus, who, in so far as they function as characters in the play, represent the solid elders of Argos. These are king's men, since the king in the heroic period stands for lawful authority; they have seen that Agamemnon's expedition was wrong, and they tell him so (799–804), but they would still be loyal to him if he were a much worse man than he is. It is these sturdy citizens who tell how, as the death reports and the urns full of ashes came in from the front, the people at home began to mutter against the king and ask why the war was fought; and, though the chorus cannot take their part, they cannot deny that there is cause for such mutterings. But the people did find a champion, or so they thought, at least a leader, Aegisthus, the king's cousin. He took advantage of the disaffection among those who hated the king he hated, and so returned from exile; he won the throne by winning the queen, confirmed his seizure by contriving the murder of Agamemnon, and defended it with his tyrant's personal bodyguard.[6]

6. The word *tyrannos* ("tyrant") was used by the Greek prose writers in a semi-technical sense, and it only gradually became a term of reproach. The tyrant was a

Thus we come about once more to the dynastic tragedy of Homer. But the interpretations of Agamemnon's murder do not exclude one another. Aeschylus can work on several levels at once. The war tragedy and the political tragedy do not contradict, they cohere with and deepen the tragedy of persons.

On the personal level, *Agamemnon* works through a complex of collisions, not so much right against wrong as right against right, each person insisting on his right with the force of passion. Agamem-

---

self-appointed despot whose career was characteristic in various places at various times in Greek history, but especially in the seventh and sixth centuries B.C. The Athenian using the word would think at once of his own tyrants, Peisistratus and his son Hippias; the restoration of the latter was still a political issue when Aeschylus was a young man. The following may serve as a general description of the typical early tyrant. He was an aristocrat, but one who was likely not to be in power while the government remained stable. He posed as a representative of the underprivileged and won and used their support, but generally got his position by unconstitutional means. His policy was generally to hold more than royal power without assuming any formal title, through influence and threat. He nevertheless always attempted to found a permanent dynasty through his sons, but hardly ever succeeded. His championship of the poorer classes was generally more than a pose, and he frequently worked toward broadening the base of democracy. Thus his most persistent enemies were not the masses but his fellow-aristocrats, except for the few he could win over into his own personal following; but, because, in spite of all the good he might do, his very existence flouted all legality, those who loved law and liberty hated him too. He had to guard himself, and infallible signs of his presence were the bodyguard of professionals and the spy system. Tyranny was one of the great growing pains in the life of young democracy, and history has been unkind to the tyrant, but for solid reasons.

Tyranny actually came later than Homeric or heroic kingship, and Aeschylus probably knew very well that it was anachronistic to see in Aegisthus' usurpation a tyrant's *coup de main*. Yet he seems to have committed that anachronism. When the chorus hear Agamemnon's death cries and sense murder by the queen and her lover, one of them says (1354–55; see also 1365): "Anyone can see it, by these first steps they have taken, they purpose to be tyrants here upon our city." In speaking of tyranny (*tyrannis*) here, either Aeschylus is using the word strictly, or he is not. He might use "tyrant" loosely, as a synonym for *basileus*, "king" (Euripides does this). But then the statement would have no point whatever, for what could the chorus expect other than that the murderer would make himself king? Plainly, they fear life not only under the wrong ruler but under the wrong kind of government. Historically, the tyrant overthrew a republic (the lawful constitution), but, in the heroic age on which tragedy drew, there was no republic; the lawful constitution was kingship; therefore, the tyrant overthrew this. When Aegisthus at last appears, he has his tyrant's bodyguard. It is impossible not to connect Aegisthus' *coup de main* with the rebellious murmuring of the masses against the king and his war. But the political pattern is a submotif, not fully worked out; its main effect is to shadow the character of Aegisthus—seducer, murderer, usurper already—with the dark memory of the hated historical tyrant.

non, the king, with a king's power and pride in arms, appears briefly
and is relatively simple. Pride would have driven him without hesi-
tation to undertake the recovery of Helen, and this decision sets in
motion a chain of events which becomes increasingly inescapable.
The sacrifice of Iphigeneia, the persistence in besieging Troy, even
the intrigue with Cassandra, follow necessarily; his pride grows on
its own acts, until just before death he is a swollen vanity. He himself
began the series of acts which pile up to overwhelm him, but, looking back, one cannot see where a proud king could have chosen
otherwise. Clytaemestra's motives are far more complex. Homer
had made her act in simple surrender and consequent betrayal. But
Pindar speculated on motives which would, if admitted by Homer,
have spoiled the cast of his version:

> Was it Iphigeneia, who at the Euripos crossing
> was slaughtered far from home,
> that vexed her to drive in anger the hand of violence?
> Or was it couching in a strange bed
> by night that broke her will and set her awry—for young wives
> a sin most vile.[7]

Two motives to choose from: Iphigeneia or Aegisthus. But Pindar
has already mentioned Cassandra and so implied a third alternative,
mother-resentment, guilty love, or jealousy. After Pindar, we could
choose A or B or C. Aeschylus ignores the "or" and takes them all.
Clytaemestra has loved Agamemnon, Iphigeneia has made her hate
him, she loves Aegisthus. But her love for Agamemnon was real, and
enough of that love remains to waken perfectly real jealousy at the
sight of Agamemnon's lovely captive. This also moves her enormous
pride, which amounts to unprecedented ambition for dynastic power.
The women of the heroic age are represented as people of character,
with will and temper of their own; but if their men insist, they must
give way. Force them and they love. Cassandra, Clytaemestra's foil
and rival, has seen her city and people wiped out by Agamemnon, her
father and brothers butchered by his followers, but she clings to him.
So Briseis in the *Iliad* clings to Achilles, who has personally killed
her husband, and so Sophocles makes his Tecmessa protest to Aias

7. Pindar *Pyth.* II. 22–25, trans. Lattimore.

that she loves him, for she has no one else, since he has destroyed her home.[8] Not so Clytaemestra, who, like Helen her sister, chooses her own loves. Again, the code obviously allowed the warlord, married or unmarried, to have the comforts of a captive mistress on campaign. But if Clytaemestra did not like a code, she would smash it. With her "male strength of heart in its high confidence," she steps boldly from the sphere of women's action into that of men;[9] like a king, she handles the city in her lord's absence, and to her the hostile and suspicious chorus turns with unwilling admiration. When the chorus doubts her intelligences, again when after the murder they openly challenge her, she faces them down and silences them; and it is only on the appearance of Aegisthus, whom they despise as they cannot despise Clytaemestra, that they break out rebelliously again. Even in deceit, as in shameless defiance, she is stately (855–88, 1667). She is the born aristocrat, heiress by birth as by marriage to the power and wealth of kings, and so contemptuous of the *nouveau riche* (1042–46). Everything she does and says is in the grand manner. The chain of beacon fires linking Argos and Troy, defeating distance and time, is a characteristically grand gesture, and worthy of it are the arrogant lines in which she concludes her story of relayed signal flares (315–16):

> By such proof and such symbol I announce to you
> my lord at Troy has sent his messengers to me.

Such is the spirit of her grandiose welcome to Agamemnon, the purple carpet on which he is forced to walk to his butchery, and the words in which such lavish outlay is defended, "the sea is there," with its plain implication that "the sea is ours."

Such characteristics give Clytaemestra stature, but in no sense justify her. It is not only that, in asserting her right, or at least determination, to act as freely as a man, she has taken to her bed the

8. The most detailed Attic study of the womanly woman in the heroic age is Euripides' Andromache in the play named after her. It is she who says (213–14): "A wife, even if she is given to a worthless man, should cling to him, not set her will up against his." It is noteworthy that her definitions of a woman's duties occur in debate with her Spartan rival, Hermione, daughter of Menelaus and Helen.

9. When she refers to herself as "a mere woman," it is with massive sarcasm (348, 590–97, 1661).

"womanish" Aegisthus. The whole house has been wrong since the quarrel of Atreus and Thyestes. Atreus was hideous in murder, but this does not justify Aegisthus in murdering Agamemnon, any more than the sins of Agamemnon justified his murder by Clytaemestra, or the sins of Paris and Helen justified the obliteration of Troy. All the executioners plead that they act for just retribution, but the chain of murder has got out of hand and is perpetuating itself, until it seems no longer to come from personal purpose but has grown into a Curse, a Thing. Every correction is a blood-bath which calls for new correction.

> The truth stands ever beside God's throne
> eternal: he who has wrought shall pay; that is law.
> Then who shall tear the curse from their blood?
> The seed is stiffened to ruin.

Clytaemestra answers, over the corpse of Agamemnon, that she has been bloody but the house is clean. No more evil need be done. Orestes is to make the same claim over the corpse of Clytaemestra herself. Both are mistaken.

The tragedy is no simple matter of right and wrong, of pride and fall, though these enter in. It is a matter of love and hate working simultaneously to force distorted action, and the situation is given depth by cross-characterization. Clytaemestra imagines before the chorus the scene in captured Troy, opening with savage satisfaction in the thought of what is going on and closing with a prayer for peace, that her husband and his men may use their victory temperately, so that no fresh wrong may follow. As she speaks these words, she is herself plotting the fresh wrong she deprecates. There is surface contradiction, but under it lies not only the fact that Clytaemestra is intensely proud of the husband she is about to murder but also the lyric imagination, akin to the diviner's gift, by which the character's mind can transcend time and distance and penetrate to a sphere of objective truth which is beyond the character's own desire and prejudice. When she tells Agamemnon and the public of the torments she went through in his absence at Troy, she is flattering him and misleading all, but by means of truth, not fiction. This is the past, and this is real.

It is evil and a thing of terror when a wife
sits in the house forlorn with no man by.

Flattery, confession, reproach combine (through how much longing
for the memory-ghost, as with Menelaus for Helen, might Clytaemestra have gone before she took Aegisthus as a lover; or even
after?). Agamemnon, on the point of being entangled by flattery
and dragged to his death, soberly describes himself as proof against
flatterers. In a sense this is irony; it corresponds to his entrance full
of the pride of capture on the heels of a warning by the chorus against
pride; to the gloomy speculations of the chorus on sackers of cities
that presages the return of the herald to tell of Troy's obliteration.
But that is mainly a matter of timing; here the point is that Agamemnon's intelligence is partly engaged with the course he does not
mean to take. He is proof against illusions except at the one point
where they will be fatal to him. When Aegisthus, in the height of
his dispute with the challenging chorus (1668), says of Orestes,

Exiles feed on empty dreams of hope. I know it. I was one,

the jibe turns into a flash of instantly forgotten sympathy. The actors, in particular Clytaemestra and the chorus, do not collide with
purely external forces but act always against a part of their own will
or sympathy which is committed to the other side, and what they kill
is what they love.

The action of the play in itself, of the trilogy as a whole, is thus
bound inward upon itself. Its course is not logical, not even strictly
dramatic sequence. After the fashion of choral lyric, it is both united
to itself and given inward dimension through persistent ideas and
a complex of symbols.

Idea and Symbol

By "idea" I mean motive, theme of subject, or type of situation
which is dominant in the dramatic action. By "symbol" I mean a
particular thing, usually material, which may be taken to represent
the idea. And by a "complex of symbols" I mean a group of such
objects which are related to one another in their nature or use.

The exhaustive study of this technique and the detailing of its uses is a proper study for a monograph, not for a segment of the introduction to a translation.[10] I will content myself with illustrating the principle through the symbol-complex of the net.

A central motive in the *Oresteia* is the idea of entanglement: the taming of wild things, the subjugation of the powerful, the involvement of innocent creatures as well. It is expressed in the *curb* forged to subdue Troy (132) or Cassandra (1066); the *bit* that gags Iphigeneia (234); the *yoke* of circumstance that forces Agamemnon to his crime; the *yoke* of slavery forced on Troy (529), on Cassandra (953, 1071, 1226), on the defiant citizens (1635), even the yoke of teammates (842); the *snare* of the huntsman, in which Agamemnon captures Troy (358, 821) and Cassandra (1048) and in which he is presently captured (1115, 1375, 1611).[11] Curb, yoke, snare—different objects for related purposes—might have been no more than persistent and thematic metaphor, but they have one embodiment which is not metaphorical, and this is the robe or shawl in which Clytaemestra actually entangles Agamemnon in order to strike him down and which is to be displayed on stage as a murder exhibit by Orestes in *The Libation Bearers* (980-84, 997-1004). Clytaemestra anticipates herself when she tells of her dreams and imaginations of terror in Agamemnon's long absence (866-68):

> Had Agamemnon taken all
> the wounds the tale whereof was carried home to me,
> he had been cut full of gashes like a fishing net,

and returns to her imagery in her challenging confession of murder (1382-83):

> as fishermen cast their huge circling nets, I spread
> deadly abundance of rich robes and caught him fast.

This is the idea seen in the thing and the thing embodying the idea, both in metaphor and in action. There are numerous other symbols and other ideas. Symbols are the snake (specially the viper) and the poison of the snake; the archer; the house; the ship; gold.

10. Miss Barbara Hughes is at present working on such a monograph as a doctoral dissertation.

11. The idea of the manhunt appears in the retributive expedition against Troy (127, 695), and in *The Eumenides* it characterizes the Furies' pursuit of Orestes.

Ideas are (in addition to entanglement) persuasion (flattery); recurrent sickness; hate-in-love; blood and sex; light in the dark; sound (of terror) in the night; dream and memory. The bare lists are not complete, and, in particular, neither symbols nor ideas are exclusive, nor does a given symbol stand toward a given idea in a one-to-one relation. The viper, who turns against his own family, whose mating is murder, stands principally for the idea of hate-in-love and, as such, might be called the prime symbol of the *Oresteia*, but its poison is involved also in the idea of recurrent sickness,[12] and its coils in the idea of entanglement (elsewhere signified by yoke, net, etc., as we have seen). So *The Libation Bearers*, 246–49:

> Behold
> the orphaned children of the eagle-father, now
> that he has died entangled in the binding coils
> of the deadly viper.

The spider web in which Agamemnon was trapped (1492) is one more variation of entanglement, spun by another creature who murders in marriage. Entanglement may come by outright force or by seduction and surprise. Clytaemestra lures Agamemnon into it by flattery, persuasion, by her sex (1116):

> Or is the trap the woman there, the murderess?

Cross-binding and coherence of idea in symbol is seen where Agamemnon recoils (he is soon to surrender) from stepping on the gorgeous robe Clytaemestra has spread at his feet (922–27)

> Such state becomes the gods, and none beside.
> I am a mortal, a man; I cannot trample down
> these tinted splendors without fear thrown in my path.
> I tell you, as a man, not god, to reverence me.
> Discordant is the murmur at such treading down
> of lovely things.

On the level of discourse, the speech is moral. The male rationalism is fighting against the irrational persuasion of the woman, the Greek defends his code ("as if I were some Asiatic"), the king deprecates the

12. The word *palinkotos* might signify a sickness or poisoning which lies hidden in the system, seemingly gone, then recurs; or the viper, which re-coils upon itself, or those so close to it that they form a part of itself.

subjects' disapproval; this is colored also by lyric memory. The "treading down of lovely things" recalls Paris, who "trampled down the delicacy of things inviolable" (371) and on whom Persuasion also worked (385). Agamemnon, who punished the barbarians, is being turned barbarian in order to be punished. He is a victim of his wife's flattery and the magnificence of his own possessions. Lastly, the robe itself on which he walks prefigures the robe in which he is to be entangled and killed.

Cut anywhere into the play, and you will find such a nexus of intercrossing motives and properties. The system gives the play its inner dimension and strength. An analogous but separable principle dominates the larger structure.

Dramatic Structure and Lyric Dimension

As theater, *Agamemnon* and its companion pieces are simple. The scene of *Agamemnon* is the familiar fixed position before the doors of a house, which is, as most often in subsequent drama and in the nature of things, a palace. The same setting serves for *The Libation Bearers; The Eumenides* has one of those shifts of scene which are relatively rare in extant Greek tragedy, for we begin before the doors of Phoebus at Delphi and end before the doors of Athene in Athens, but this shift can easily be signified by addition or subtraction of a very few properties.

Characters are used sparingly. Aeschylus has at his disposal the three actors who were by now allotted to each poet or producer; but, far from reveling in this sober allowance, he is most reluctant to use all three at once in speaking action. Cassandra is on stage with Agamemnon and Clytaemestra, but does not speak until the other actors (not counting the chorus or chorus leader) have gone out.[13] Dialogue is, for the most part, just that, a passage between

13. Clytaemestra, apparently on stage at 83, does not respond to the chorus at that point and remains silent through their stasimon (ode); she speaks only when, 258-63, they address her again. In *The Libation Bearers* Pylades, present almost through the entire play, speaks only three lines (900-902); these have critical force in the action. In *Prometheus*, the titan is silent all through the first scene, where he is being fastened to the rock. We know also that Aeschylus exploited the silent character in many of

two persons, one of whom may be the chorus leader, at a time, not as in modern drama a complex in which three, four, or a dozen speaking persons participate. There are supernumeraries to be sure, handmaidens attending Clytaemestra and soldiers returning with Agamemnon, the significant bodyguard of Aegisthus; and at the close of *The Eumenides* the stage is quite full of people, and the exodus takes on the dignity of a processional. Agamemnon clearly must enter with Cassandra beside him in a horse-drawn chariot. The unrolling of the robe for Agamemnon's feet is an effective use of showy gesture. Yet, on the whole, the trilogy is physically unpretentious, relying less on staging and properties than *Prometheus* appears to do. Also, it is physically static; not much physical activity or motion is called for. The use made of materials, of what might appeal to the eye, is measured and temperate.

There is a corresponding simplicity in plot. Considering the length of *Agamemnon*, there are few events that take place, nor are the major events displayed against any variety of subplot. It therefore takes dramatic time for these events to happen. The return of Aga-

---

his lost plays. On the silent characters of Aeschylus, see the scene in the *Frogs* of Aristophanes, where the ghost of Euripides challenges that of Aeschylus in the presence of Dionysus and Hades (911–22):

"*Eur.*: First of all he would cover a character's face and make him sit on the stage there,
Achilles, maybe, or Niobe, but never show their features.
They made his tragedy look fine, but didn't mutter a syllable.

"*Dion.*: By god, you know, they didn't at that.

"*Eur.*:   The chorus would pound out long chains of poetry, four one after another. The characters said nothing.

"*Dion.*: You know, I liked them quiet that way. They gave me as much pleasure as the ones that gabble at us now.

"*Eur.*:   Of course. You were a half-wit and that's a fact.

"*Dion.*:   I know, I know. Tell me then, why did he do it?

"*Eur.*: To lead you on, and keep the audience in suspense. They were waiting for Niobe to speak. Meanwhile his play was getting over.

"*Dion.*: The dirty rat! So all that time he was cheating us out of our drama. (*To Aesch.*) Why are you frowning and looking so cross?

"*Eur.*:   I'm exposing him. He doesn't like it."

memnon, assured from the watchman's opening speech (25), does not take place until line 782.[14] The only other *event* of the play is his murder, which does not take place until line 1344. Audience and actors occupy the times preceding these events in a growing strain of suspense, which gives the events redoubled impact when at last they do take place. The means by which the anomaly of many lines–little action is solved are the same as the means by which action and motive are deepened. The simplicity is on the surface. As, on its major plane, the action of the tragedy moves deliberately forward, in another dimension lyric memory and forecast take us, by association of ideas rather than in obedience to order in time, deep away into the past, the future, and the elsewhere.

Memory and forecast are a part of imagination, that divining spirit which takes men beyond the limits of what their senses can perceive. He who habitually, and under patronage of a god, so divines is the *mantis* or prophet. The prophet knew "all things that

14. Much unnecessary ingenuity has been wasted on the problem of "real" time in *Agamemnon*. By means of her beacons, Clytaemestra is understood to learn of Troy's capture just after the event, almost within the hour (320). The return voyage from Troy to Argos is a three or four days' sailing, hardly shortened by the hurricane that wrecked the fleet; and, further, Homer and the other sources on which tragedy drew make it plain that the Achaeans did not pick up and go home the moment Troy fell but understandably took some time getting off. Therefore, the arrival of the herald, followed by Agamemnon, comes days after the first scene of the play. This is true, but creates a problem only for those unduly preoccupied with the Aristotelian unities. "Tragedy tries as far as practicable to fall within the scope of a single day, or exceeds it by only a little" (*Poetics* v. 8). The statement of Aristotle is not made as if he meant to press it very hard. Also it should not be necessary, but apparently is, to point out that Aeschylus had never heard of Aristotle. To Aeschylus, the next thing that happened *in the plot*, after the arrival of the news, was the arrival of the Achaeans. It would have been, to him, as pointless as it would have been ugly to have the chorus solemnly quit the stage and return after the posting of a placard saying "six days later." What he does put in is a long choral lyric in which the choristers muse on the whole train of action (though not in chronological order) from the flight of Helen to the fall of Troy; thus giving in lyric form the illusion that far more time has passed than the real time it has actually taken them to deliver their ode. At l. 475, after the lyric closes, they begin to speak "in character." Their mood has changed; before the ode they were utterly convinced by Clytaemestra's beacons; now they are unconvinced and sarcastic. After the herald's speeches, they inform Clytaemestra that she has been right all along, and she tells them she has done *her* rejoicing *long ago*. By now, we are plainly meant to understand that a lapse of time has occurred, but *not* encouraged to figure out just how much, or how it could have happened.

were, the things to come, and the things past" (*Iliad* i. 70); that is, he knew not only past and future, but *present*, what is occurring right now beyond that fragmentary point of space where he stands. Calchas the prophet of the Achaeans is remembered in the first ode, Cassandra the prophetess of Troy appears in person. But, apart from these formal prophets, the chorus assumes divining powers ("still by God's grace there surges within me singing magic": "why this strain unwanted, unrepaid, thus prophetic?"), and the imaginations of Clytaemestra, the herald, Agamemnon, and Aegisthus range far away. Calchas, in the memory of the chorus, goes deep into the past in order to make predictions which will be fulfilled, years away, in the subsequent action of the tragedy. Cassandra, who knows of a past she never witnessed, sees in its light the invisible network of treachery that waits for Agamemnon and her. The swan, who sings in the face of death and is helplessly dedicated to Apollo, is her symbol.

The choristers remember in their entrance chant the departure of the armament ten years ago (40–59), and it makes them see the struggle going on in Troy (60–68). They remember the portents that attended the gathering of the ships, the predictions of Calchas, and the sacrifice of Iphigeneia that was their sequel (104–257). Clytaemestra's living imagination follows the course of her beacon system, itself a device to defeat space and diminish time, as it breaks out from peak to peak on its way to her (281–316), and she sees the Achaeans in captured Troy, now, though far away (320–37). The chorus broods on the moral that Troy fallen conveys, but they think in pictures; of a man secure in wealth kicking over an altar (the audience will remember the golden Persians, their pride, sacrilege, and defeat); of Persuasion as a siren; of false fires and spurious metal gilded; of a greedy innocent child trying to catch a bird—the images, not the propositions, of delusion (367–95). This is Paris, and they fall at once to re-creating in imagination the flight of Helen (403–8). And there were *prophets* there, to be sure, who imagined the loneliness to follow for Menelaus with an empty bed and empty-eyed images of his wife, whose loveliness eluded him in dreams (408–26). But dream image is memory image, and there are others who remember too. The families of the common soldiers see brought back to them the ashes of their dead, transubstantiated by the money-changer, who is the god of war. They murmur against the king; their muttering is inarticulate and not clearly heard in high places but may be the symptom of a storm that waits for the returning king (427–74). *Te deum laudamus* has been transformed into foreboding, not through logical succession of ground and consequent but through a lyric succession of images whose forms melt into one another. Agamemnon's herald remembers the campaigning before Troy (551–81). At first, it is the dirty and brutal details of war-business that come out of the mist, but the sense of achievement infects him with Agamemnon's fatal pride, so that at the end the wings of his imagination take him out of the past across the present and far into the future and the days when the capture of Troy will be an antique glory of Argos. He is shaken out of this mood, however, by the questioning of the chorus leader, who wants to know what happened to the rest of the army and to Menelaus. He tells of the storm (650–70) in terms that make living things out of fire, wind, water, and rocks, and shows the wide seascape on which at dawn lay the wreckage of the Achaean fleet, torn flowers on the water.

The chorus, far now from the momentary exaltation they felt at news of the victory, now chant in terms of disaster: the sinister name of Helen, with the imagination once again of her flight to Troy (681–98); the lion's cub, the pet turned murderous (716–36), who is fatal Helen beguiling the Trojans (737–49). We remember Iphigeneia when Helen's eyes, like Iphigeneia's, sweep the beholder with soft arrows, and the victorious and guileful charmer recalls the innocent charmer who failed. The moralities which follow to prelude Agamemnon's entrance, the terms in which he is greeted, work again through images: houses gilded to hide dust, false coin, the smile of the charmer. Action follows in the public encounter of Clytaemestra and Agamemnon, but the wife's welcome brings back out of the past the fears that attended her during the years of separation (858–94). When he has gone into the house, the chorus turn uneasily from memory to forecast, and their gloom is abetted by Cassandra, who has vision on vision of the past, of the present (the intention behind

Clytaemestra's face and words, the scene preparing behind closed doors), and the far future on the day when the avengers shall punish for the crime not yet committed (1069–1330). The death cry tells the chorus only what they already know. We do not see the murder take place, but we are told what happened (1381–92). In the scene that follows, where Clytaemestra faces the people, neither side can escape the memory of the hideous past which has forced these things to happen. Aegisthus' defense is a recounting of the crime of Atreus (1583–1611). At the end, Clytaemestra speaks as if all were over, but we know it is not, that the future holds more violence and it is the past which has made this so.

Lyric Tragedy

The brief dramatic time of the play is a point of convergence for actions that come from deep in the past and project far into the future. The limited stage is a pivotal point from which we can be transported far away. The tragedy of Agamemnon, Cassandra, and Clytaemestra is involved with and opens into the tragedy of the children of Thyestes, of Iphigeneia, of Troy and all the Achaean army; and its action, in return, is partly dictated by the figures never enacted, remote but always present in memory, of Atreus, Iphigeneia, Paris, and Helen.[15]

This is the form of lyric tragedy, perfected here and never since so completely realized. Its manner is due partly to the historical accident in which two forms of fiction were combined: drama, still relatively primitive and naïve, with choral lyric, now, after generations of mature practice, brought to its highest point of development by Simonides and Pindar. But the direction taken by this form is due also to deliberate choice. The desire is to transcend the limitations of dramatic presentation, even before these limitations have been firmly established. The spirit is that of Shakespeare's chorus in *Henry V:*

15. We may compare *The Persians*. The cast of actors consists only of Darius, his queen, Xerxes, messenger, and chorus. The visible scene in Persia is static. But the scene of the action which the play is *about* is Salamis, and then all the water and land between; the persons of this action are all the vast army of the Persians, and all the Greeks. *The Persians* is the great messenger-play.

> But pardon, gentles all,
> The flat unraised spirits that have dared
> On this unworthy scaffold to bring forth
> So great an object: can this cockpit hold
> The vasty fields of France? Or may we cram
> Within this wooden O the very casques
> That did affright the air at Agincourt?

It is true that Shakespeare intends to take us to the actual field of Agincourt, but principally he is aware of the impossibility of *staging* expeditions and battles adequately, and the appeal is to the imagination of the audience:

> For 'tis your thoughts that now must deck our kings,
> Carry them here and there; jumping o'er times,
> Turning the accomplishment of many years
> Into an hour-glass.

> Thus with imagined wing our swift scene flies
> In motion of no less celerity
> Than that of thought.

Shakespeare and Aeschylus alike forecast combinations which only the motion picture can realize visually—flashback, imaginary scene, pictorial dramatization of history, and messenger's account. Shakespeare's concern in this particular play with the fragmentary nature of staged action gives his chorus a brilliant part, but it is only a ghost of Aeschylus, for in Aeschylus the past and the elsewhere dominate present action.

But the direction in which he steered tragedy was not generally followed. Sophoclean drama prevailed, since Euripides, under protest, framed tragedy in accordance with Sophocles, not Aeschylus. Sophocles turned tragedy inward upon the principal actors, and drama becomes drama of character. His plays may open with public scenes, but, as they progress, the interest focuses hard on the hero. *Oedipus Tyrannus* begins with the plague in Thebes, but its ending is all Oedipus, and Thebes is as good as forgotten. It is true that the dead hand reaches out of the past to strike down Oedipus, Antigone, Aias, Heracles. But this is their tragedy, and theirs alone. *Agamemnon* is a play about the Trojan War, but *Antigone* is not a play about the

Theban War, though that lies in the background. In Sophocles, the choruses are commentaries on the action, not part of the larger action, and their imagery is functional to the choruses themselves but not to the tragedy as a whole. Trilogy gives way to single drama. The enormous background becomes mainly irrelevant and is screened out. Lyric tragedy gives way to actor's tragedy.

Agamemnon is, in fact, the culmination of lyric tragedy, because the action narrows in *The Libation Bearers*, and when in *The Eumenides* it opens out again, it is with a new kind of meaning and composition.

"The Libation Bearers"

The second play of the trilogy takes place some years after the close of *Agamemnon*. The usurpers have grown secure in power. Orestes, sequestered in Phocis, is now a young man, and his sister Electra, resentful and bitter, awaits his return. The opening event is simple recognition, the identification of Orestes and the confirmation of the fact that, as Electra and the chorus hope, he means to avenge his father and regain his throne. Recognition is thus at once transformed into conspiracy. The children, with their faithful chorus, gather at Agamemnon's tomb, where Electra has gone on her mother's behalf, but without sympathy for her, to propitiate the dead king by reason of terrifying dreams which had shaken Clytaemestra in the night. The dead king is now a hero; his arrogance and his mistakes have been annulled by death, and his grave is a center of power. Therefore, the children with the chorus turn to him, invoke his ghost to anger against his murderers, with twofold driving intention: to enchant actual power out of the spirit and the grave and to incite themselves and arm themselves with the anger that will make them do what they must do. They then plot the means for assassination. Orestes poses as a traveling merchant who brings news of the death of Orestes; Clytaemestra, with archaic and stately courtesy, invites him in and sends for Aegisthus. As the messenger who is sent to summon him (she happens to be the slave who nursed Orestes when he was little) goes out on her errand, she encounters the chorus, who tell her not to suggest that Aegisthus should bring his bodyguard. Orestes and Pylades kill the king, and Clytaemestra stands at their mercy. She dares Orestes to kill her, and he stands irresolute until a word from Pylades solidifies his will. The bodies are brought out and displayed, with the robe in which Agamemnon had been entrapped, and Orestes declares publicly, as Clytaemestra had done, that this act is his own and that it is justice. But his wits are going, he sees the Furies, the avenging spirits of his mother (no one else can see them), and leaves in flight. This time, even before the play is over, the assassin knows that his act was not final but has created more suffering yet to come.

Once again the plot is simple, and the dramatic actions are few. Once again, despite these facts, the texture is saved from thinness, but the factors are different from those that give *Agamemnon* its coherence. First, this is a far shorter play. Second, the emphasis and direction have changed. We have, in a sense, more plot; there is intrigue, a practical problem. In *Agamemnon* the king's murder is felt by the witnessing chorus in their bones; it happens, is mourned, and defended. The problems of Clytaemestra, *whether* she can kill the husband she has loved and *how* she will do it, are implicit, but we are not present while she is solving them. But in *The Libation Bearers*, we are present at the deliberations of Orestes as he decides whether he can kill his mother, and how the assassination is to be effected. In recognition, decision, conspiracy, and climactic action we have, in fact, the mechanism, in naïve or even crude form, of that drama of revenge or play of successful action which we found in the Homeric story.

But *The Libation Bearers* is only superficially a drama of intrigue, and, in so far as it is one, it is hardly a significant specimen of its kind. The mechanism of the assassin's plot is simple, as the mechanism of recognition and identification is primitive. The emphasis lies on the mood in which the characters act.

For this is not a simple revenge play in which the young hero, long lost, returns to his sister and his kingdom to strike down the murderous and usurping villains. Orestes hardly gets a sight of his kingship before he must leave, haunted, driven, and alone. It is not until much later, near the close of *The Eumenides*, that he can speak

as a king with subjects. Also, here the emotions of Orestes and Electra are, like those of Clytaemestra, half-committed to the side against
which they act; and Clytaemestra, in turn, loves the son whom she
fears, who kills her, and whom she would kill if she could. It is the
philos-aphilos still, or love-in-hate, the murder committed not against
an external enemy but against a part of the self.[16] The hate gains in-
tensity from the strength of the original love when that love has
been stopped or rejected. Electra ("the unmarried") has love to
lavish, but her mother has turned it aside. The chorus, like the captive women they are, cling to the memory of Agamemnon, who enslaved them. Orestes, together with the sense of outrage over the
loss of his rightful inheritance (the dynastic motive), nurses a deep
sense of jealousy against his mother for having sacrificed not only
Agamemnon but *Orestes* to her love for Aegisthus. The children
were the price for which she bought herself this man (132–34). It is
the venom of such jealousy that spills out in the bitterly salacious
mockery of the dead lovers, and jealousy on his father's behalf and
his own is the theme of his last sharp dispute with his mother. Clytaemestra, when she hears the false news of her son's death, is in a
temper where relief and sorrow cross, though relief wins. Her very
dream of bearing and nursing the snake (symbol of ingratitude), who
fixes his poisonous fangs in her breast, enacts terror through a gesture of love. Aegisthus, at the word that Orestes is dead, goes soberly
back to the image of the poison and the snake:

> For our house, already bitten
> and poisoned, to take this new load upon itself
> would be a thing of dripping fear and blood.

The chorus consider that both the tyrants are hypocrites, but even
such hypocrites know what they are doing, and to whom.

This mood of tangled motivation means that the conspirators
must work strongly upon themselves before they can act. Between
the recognition and the resolve to act comes a scene of incantation.

16. So *Hamlet* is transformed from the vigorous revenge-intrigue drama it might
have been into the tragedy it is, because Hamlet is emotionally involved with the queen
and Ophelia, who are on the side of the enemy. Even the arch-enemy is close in blood
and perhaps once admired.

Sister, brother, and chorus turn to invoke dead Agamemnon. They implore his blessings and aid, they set forth their grievances and his, they challenge and taunt him to action:

Orestes

Think of that bath, father, where you were stripped of life.

Electra

Think of the casting-net that they contrived for you.

Orestes

They caught you like a beast in toils no bronzesmith made.

Electra

Rather, hid you in shrouds that were thought out in shame.

Orestes

Will you not waken, father to these challenges?

Electra

Will you not rear upright that best beloved head?

But, while they are invoking a power and a tradition whose force is felt but only dimly believed, they are also lashing themselves into the fury of self-pity that will make them do what they have to do. So the theme of lyric prophecy which was at work in *Agamemnon* is altered here. There is dealing in both cases with what lies beyond the powers of perception, but there it was lyric memory and vision on the part of those who were to witness, and to suffer from, the ugly act; here those who are themselves about to commit the ugly act manipulate the unseen, in a mood more of witchcraft than of prophecy.

For this reason and because the drama focuses on the will to act, *The Libation Bearers* ties back to *Agamemnon*, but *Agamemnon* ties back to the whole world of action latent behind the beginning of the tragedy. The symbols of the earlier play are caught up and intensified, particularly viper and net. But the emphasis is changed, because we see things from the point of view of the murderers. In *Agamemnon*, vice was alluring, wearing all the captivating graces of Helen and her attendant symbols; in *The Libation Bearers*, duty becomes repulsive. Both tragedies are carried on a strong underdrift of sex, but in the second play the sex impulse, though it works, has lost its charm. Orestes at the end has done a brutal, necessary job.

Like Clytaemestra at the close of *Agamemnon*, Orestes defends his position in terms of: "I have cleared my house. It was bloody, but necessary. Now we can have peace." As for Clytaemestra, his claim is no better than a desperate challenge flung at circumstances. The blood-bath was no cleaning-out, and it means more blood. Clytaemestra had to reckon with resentment in the state and the younger generation to come. The enlightenment of Orestes, the defeat of his hollow optimism, comes without delay. "The house has been rid of snakes": and at once, on the heads of his mother's Furies, more snakes appear.

"*The Eumenides*" (*The Furies*)

As we have seen (see above, p. 6), the last act of the trilogy finds Orestes cleared by Apollo but still pursued by the Furies. Is he clear, or not? Plainly, one divine decision has clashed with another decision which is also unquestionably divine. The fate of Orestes is referred to Athens and to a third divinity, Athene, who, reserving for herself the casting ballot, refers it to a jury of mortal men. When their vote is even and Athene has cast her deciding vote in his favor, the Furies must be propitiated by a new cult, as a new kind of goddess, in Athens. It is this episode that closes the play and the trilogy of the House of Atreus. The chorus has returned to its archaic part as chief character in the drama.

Who are the Furies, and what do they mean? And, since they stand up and identify themselves and protest their rights in the face of Apollo and Athene, we must also ask, What do these better-known Olympians represent for the purposes of Aeschylus?

As seen in the grand perspective, Agamemnon was only an unwilling agent in a chain of action far bigger than the fortunes of a single man. From the seduction of Atreus' wife, the murder of the children of Thyestes, the sacrifice of Iphigeneia and the youth of Hellas, claim and counterclaim have been fiercely sustained, each act of blood has been avenged in a new act of blood. The problems of public good have been solved through private murder, which is no solution, until the situation has become intolerable to the forces that rule the world, and these must intervene to see that the contestants and the impulses in nature which drive the contestants become reconciled and find their places in a scheme that will be harmonious and progressive, not purely destructive.

Behind the personal motivations in the two first dramas of the trilogy, we can, if we choose, discern a conflict of related forces: of the younger against the elder generation; of male against female; of Greek against barbarian. As the gods step out of the darkness, where, before, they could be reached only in fitful visions of the prophetic mind, and take their place on the stage, they personify these general forces, and, because they are divine and somewhat abstract, they can carry still further dimensions of meaning. The Furies are older than Apollo and Athene, and, being older, they are childish and barbarous; attached to Clytaemestra as mother, they are themselves female and represent the woman's claim to act which Clytaemestra has sustained from the beginning; in a Greek world they stand for the childhood of the race before it won Hellenic culture, the barbarian phase of pre-Hellenism, the dark of the race and of the world; they have archaic uprightness and strictness in action, with its attendant cruelty; they insist on the fact against the idea; they ignore the justifications of Orestes, for the blood on his hands means far more than the reasons why the blood is there. Apollo stands for everything which the Furies are not: Hellenism, civilization, intellect, and enlightenment. He is male and young. He despises cruelty for the fun of cruelty, and the thirst for blood, but he is as ruthless as the Furies. The commonwealth of the gods—therefore the universe—is in a convulsion of growth; the young Olympians are fighting down their own barbaric past.

But they must not fight it out of existence. In the impasse, Apollo uses every threat of arrogant force, but Athene, whose nature reconciles female with male, has a wisdom deeper than the intelligence of Apollo. She clears Orestes but concedes to the detested Furies what they had not known they wanted, a place in the affections of a civilized community of men, as well as in the divine hierarchy. There, gracious and transformed though they are, their place in the world is still made potent by the unchanged base of their character.

The new city cannot progress by exterminating its old order of life; it must absorb and use it. Man cannot obliterate, and should not repress, the unintelligible emotions. Or again, in different terms, man's nature being what it is and Fury being a part of it, Justice must go armed with Terror before it can work.

Thus, through the dilemma of Orestes and its solution, the drama of the House of Atreus has been transformed into a grand parable of progress. Persuasion (flattery), the deadly magic of the earlier plays, has been turned to good by Athene as she wins the Furies to accept of their own free will a new and better place in the world. By the time Orestes leaves the stage, he has become an issue, a Dred Scott or Dreyfus, more important for what he means than for what he is; and, when he goes, the last human personality is gone, and with it vanish the bloody entanglements of the House of Atreus, as the anonymous citizens of Athens escort their protecting divinities into the beginning of a new world.

It is appropriate, and characteristic of Aeschylus, that this final parable, with its tremendous burden of thought, should be enacted on the frame of a naïve dramatic structure, where the basis of decision on matricide is as crude as the base of Portia's decision against Shylock. The magnificence of *The Eumenides* is different from that of *Agamemnon*. The imagery—the lyric imagination in memory and magic—is gone, because we are not now merely to see but to understand. The final act comes down into the present day and seals within itself the wisdom, neither reactionary nor revolutionary, of a great man. But in its own terms *The Eumenides* is the necessary conclusion of a trilogy whose special greatness lies in the fact that it transcends the limitations of dramatic enactment on a scale never achieved before or since.

AGAMEMNON

CHARACTERS

Watchman

Clytaemestra

Herald

Agamemnon

Cassandra

Aegisthus

Chorus of Argive Elders

*Attendants of Clytaemestra: of Agamemnon: bodyguard
of Aegisthus (all silent parts)*

Time, directly after the fall of Troy.

AGAMEMNON

SCENE: *Argos, before the palace of King Agamemnon. The Watchman,*
who speaks the opening lines, is posted on the roof of the palace.
Clytaemestra's entrances are made from a door in the center of the
stage; all others, from the wings.

(*The Watchman, alone.*)

I ask the gods some respite from the weariness
of this watchtime measured by years I lie awake
elbowed upon the Atreidae's roof dogwise to mark
the grand processionals of all the stars of night
burdened with winter and again with heat for men,   5
dynasties in their shining blazoned on the air,
these stars, upon their wane and when the rest arise.

I wait; to read the meaning in that beacon light,
a blaze of fire to carry out of Troy the rumor
and outcry of its capture; to such end a lady's   10
male strength of heart in its high confidence ordains.
Now as this bed stricken with night and drenched with dew
I keep, nor ever with kind dreams for company:
since fear in sleep's place stands forever at my head
against strong closure of my eyes, or any rest: 15
I mince such medicine against sleep failed: I sing,
only to weep again the pity of this house
no longer, as once, administered in the grand way.
Now let there be again redemption from distress,
the flare burning from the blackness in good augury.   20

(*A light shows in the distance.*)

Oh hail, blaze of the darkness, harbinger of day's
shining, and of processionals and dance and choirs
of multitudes in Argos for this day of grace.
Ahoy!
I cry the news aloud to Agamemnon's queen,   25

that she may rise up from her bed of state with speed
to raise the rumor of gladness welcoming this beacon,
and singing rise, if truly the citadel of Ilium
has fallen, as the shining of this flare proclaims.
I also, I, will make my choral prelude, since 30
my lord's dice cast aright are counted as my own,
and mine the tripled sixes of this torchlit throw.

May it only happen. May my king come home, and I
take up within this hand the hand I love. The rest
I leave to silence; for an ox stands huge upon 35
my tongue. The house itself, could it take voice, might speak
aloud and plain. I speak to those who understand,
but if they fail, I have forgotten everything.

(Exit. The Chorus enters, speaking.)

Ten years since the great contestants 40
of Priam's right,
Menelaus and Agamemnon, my lord,
twin throned, twin sceptered, in twofold power
of kings from God, the Atreidae,
put forth from this shore 45
the thousand ships of the Argives,
the strength and the armies.
Their cry of war went shrill from the heart,
as eagles stricken in agony
for young perished, high from the nest 50
eddy and circle
to bend and sweep of the wings' stroke,
lost far below
the fledgelings, the nest, and the tendance.
Yet someone hears in the air, a god, 55
Apollo, Pan, or Zeus, the high
thin wail of these sky-guests, and drives
late to its mark
the Fury upon the transgressors.

So drives Zeus the great guest god

the Atreidae against Alexander:
for one woman's promiscuous sake
the struggling masses, legs tired,
knees grinding in dust,
spears broken in the onset.   65
Danaans and Trojans
they have it alike. It goes as it goes
now. The end will be destiny.
You cannot burn flesh or pour unguents,
not innocent cool tears,   70
that will soften the gods' stiff anger.

But we; dishonored, old in our bones,
cast off even then from the gathering horde,
stay here, to prop up
on staves the strength of a baby.   75
Since the young vigor that urges
inward to the heart
is frail as age, no warcraft yet perfect,
while beyond age, leaf
withered, man goes three footed   80
no stronger than a child is,
a dream that falters in daylight.

      (Clytaemestra enters quietly. The Chorus continues to speak.)
But you, lady,
daughter of Tyndareus, Clytaemestra, our queen:
What is there to be done? What new thing have you heard?   85
In persuasion of what
report do you order such sacrifice?
To all the gods of the city,
the high and the deep spirits,
to them of the sky and the market places,   90
the altars blaze with oblations.
The staggered flame goes sky high
one place, then another,
drugged by the simple soft

persuasion of sacred unguents,   95
the deep stored oil of the kings.
Of these things what can be told
openly, speak.
Be healer to this perplexity
that grows now into darkness of thought,   100
while again sweet hope shining from the flames
beats back the pitiless pondering
of sorrow that eats my heart.

I have mastery yet to chant the wonder at the wayside
given to kings. Still by God's grace there surges within me   105
singing magic
grown to my life and power,
how the wild bird portent
hurled forth the Achaeans'
twin-stemmed power single hearted,   110
lords of the youth of Hellas,
with spear and hand of strength
to the land of Teucrus.
Kings of birds to the kings of the ships,
one black, one blazed with silver,   115
clear seen by the royal house
on the right, the spear hand,
they lighted, watched by all
tore a hare, ripe, bursting with young unborn yet,
stayed from her last fleet running.   120
Sing sorrow, sorrow: but good win out in the end.

Then the grave seer of the host saw through to the hearts divided,
knew the fighting sons of Atreus feeding on the hare
with the host, their people.
Seeing beyond, he spoke: 125
"With time, this foray
shall stalk the castle of Priam.
Before then, under
the walls, Fate shall spoil

in violence the rich herds of the people.   130
Only let no doom of the gods darken
upon this huge iron forged to curb Troy—
from inward. Artemis the undefiled
is angered with pity
at the flying hounds of her father   135
eating the unborn young in the hare and the shivering mother.
She is sick at the eagles' feasting.
Sing sorrow, sorrow: but good win out in the end.

Lovely you are and kind   140
to the tender young of ravening lions.
For sucklings of all the savage
beasts that lurk in the lonely places you have sympathy.
Grant meaning to these appearances
good, yet not without evil.   145
Healer Apollo, I pray you
let her not with cross winds
bind the ships of the Danaans
to time-long anchorage   150
forcing a second sacrifice unholy, untasted,
working bitterness in the blood
and faith lost. For the terror returns like sickness to lurk in the
     house;
the secret anger remembers the child that shall be avenged."   155
Such, with great good things beside, rang out in the voice of
     Calchas,
these fatal signs from the birds by the way to the house of the
     princes,
wherewith in sympathy
sing sorrow, sorrow: but good win out in the end.

Zeus: whatever he may be, if this name   160
pleases him in invocation,
thus I call upon him.
I have pondered everything
yet I cannot find a way,

only Zeus, to cast this dead weight of ignorance   165
finally from out my brain.

He who in time long ago was great,
throbbing with gigantic strength,
shall be as if he never were, unspoken.   170
He who followed him has found
his master, and is gone.
Cry aloud without fear the victory of Zeus,
you will not have failed the truth: 175

Zeus, who guided men to think,
who has laid it down that wisdom
comes alone through suffering.
Still there drips in sleep against the heart
grief of memory; against   180
our pleasure we are temperate.
From the gods who sit in grandeur
grace comes somehow violent.

On that day the elder king
of the Achaean ships, no more
strict against the prophet's word,   185
turned with the crosswinds of fortune,
when no ship sailed, no pail was full,
and the Achaean people sulked
fast against the shore at Aulis
facing Chalcis, where the tides ebb and surge: 190

and winds blew from the Strymon, bearing
sick idleness, ships tied fast, and hunger,
distraction of the mind, carelessness
for hull and cable;   195
with time's length bent to double measure
by delay crumbled the flower and pride
of Argos. Then against the bitter wind
the seer's voice clashed out
another medicine   200

more hateful yet, and spoke of Artemis, so that the kings
dashed their staves to the ground and could not hold their tears.

The elder lord spoke aloud before them: 205
"My fate is angry if I disobey these,
but angry if I slaughter
this child, the beauty of my house,
with maiden blood shed staining
these father's hands beside the altar.   210
What of these things goes now without disaster?
How shall I fail my ships
and lose my faith of battle?
For them to urge such sacrifice of innocent blood   215
angrily, for their wrath is great—it is right. May all be well yet."

But when necessity's yoke was put upon him
he changed, and from the heart the breath came bitter
and sacrilegious, utterly infidel,   220
to warp a will now to be stopped at nothing.
The sickening in men's minds, tough,
reckless in fresh cruelty brings daring. He endured then
to sacrifice his daughter
to stay the strength of war waged for a woman,   225
first offering for the ships' sake.

Her supplications and her cries of father
were nothing, nor the child's lamentation
to kings passioned for battle.   230
The father prayed, called to his men to lift her
with strength of hand swept in her robes aloft
and prone above the altar, as you might lift
a goat for sacrifice, with guards
against the lips' sweet edge, to check   235
the curse cried on the house of Atreus
by force of bit and speech drowned in strength.

Pouring then to the ground her saffron mantle
she struck the sacrificers with   240
the eyes' arrows of pity,

lovely as in a painted scene, and striving
to speak—as many times
at the kind festive table of her father
she had sung, and in the clear voice of a stainless maiden 245
with love had graced the song
of worship when the third cup was poured.

What happened next I saw not, neither speak it.
The crafts of Calchas fail not of outcome.
Justice so moves that those only learn 250
who suffer; and the future
you shall know when it has come; before then, forget it.
It is grief too soon given.
All will come clear in the next dawn's sunlight.
Let good fortune follow these things as 255
she who is here desires,
our Apian land's singlehearted protectress.

(*The Chorus now turns toward Clytaemestra, and the leader
speaks to her.*)

I have come in reverence, Clytaemestra, of your power.
For when the man is gone and the throne void, his right
falls to the prince's lady, and honor must be given. 260
Is it some grace—or otherwise—that you have heard
to make you sacrifice at messages of good hope?
I should be glad to hear, but must not blame your silence.

Clytaemestra

As it was said of old, may the dawn child be born
to be an angel of blessing from the kindly night. 265
You shall know joy beyond all you ever hoped to hear.
The men of Argos have taken Priam's citadel.

Chorus

What have you said? Your words escaped my unbelief.

Clytaemestra

The Achaeans are in Troy. Is that not clear enough?

Chorus

This slow delight steals over me to bring forth tears.   270

Clytaemestra

Yes, for your eyes betray the loyal heart within.

Chorus

Yet how can I be certain? Is there some evidence?

Clytaemestra

There is, there must be; unless a god has lied to me.

Chorus

Is it dream visions, easy to believe, you credit?

Clytaemestra

I acccpt nothing from a brain that is dull with sleep.   275

Chorus

The charm, then, of some rumor, that made rich your hope?

Clytaemestra

Am I some young girl, that you find my thoughts so silly?

Chorus

How long, then, is it since the citadel was stormed?

Clytaemestra

It is the night, the mother of this dawn I hailed.

Chorus

What kind of messenger could come in speed like this?   280

Clytaemestra

Hephaestus, who cast forth the shining blaze from Ida.
And beacon after beacon picking up the flare
carried it here; Ida to the Hermaean horn
of Lemnos, where it shone above the isle, and next
the sheer rock face of Zeus on Athos caught it up;   285
and plunging skyward to arch the shoulders of the sea
the strength of the running flare in exultation,
pine timbers flaming into gold, like the sunrise,

brought the bright message to Macistus' sentinel cliffs,
who, never slow nor in the carelessness of sleep   290
caught up, sent on his relay in the courier chain,
and far across Euripus' streams the beacon flare
carried to signal watchmen on Messapion.
These took it again in turn, and heaping high a pile
of silvery brush flamed it to throw the message on.   295
And the flare sickened never, but grown stronger yet
outleapt the river valley of Asopus like
the very moon for shining, to Cithaeron's scaur
to waken the next station of the flaming post.
These watchers, not contemptuous of the far-thrown blaze,   300
kindled another beacon vaster than commanded.
The light leaned high above Gorgopis' staring marsh,
and striking Aegyplanctus' mountain top, drove on
yet one more relay, lest the flare die down in speed.
Kindled once more with stintless heaping force, they send   305
the beard of flame to hugeness, passing far beyond
the promontory that gazes on the Saronic strait
and flaming far, until it plunged at last to strike
the steep rock of Arachnus near at hand, our watchtower.
And thence there fell upon this house of Atreus' sons   310
the flare whose fathers mount to the Idaean beacon.
These are the changes on my torchlight messengers,
one from another running out the laps assigned.
The first and the last sprinters have the victory.
By such proof and such symbol I announce to you   315
my lord at Troy has sent his messengers to me.

Chorus

The gods, lady, shall have my prayers and thanks straightway.
And yet to hear your story till all wonder fades
would be my wish, could you but tell it once again.

Clytaemestra

The Achaeans have got Troy, upon this very day.   320
I think the city echoes with a clash of cries.

Pour vinegar and oil into the selfsame bowl,
you could not say they mix in friendship, but fight on.
Thus variant sound the voices of the conquerors
and conquered, from the opposition of their fates.   325
Trojans are stooping now to gather in their arms
their dead, husbands and brothers; children lean to clasp
the aged who begot them, crying upon the death
of those most dear, from lips that never will be free.
The Achaeans have their midnight work after the fighting   330
that sets them down to feed on all the city has,
ravenous, headlong, by no rank and file assigned,
but as each man has drawn his shaken lot by chance.
And in the Trojan houses that their spears have taken
they settle now, free of the open sky, the frosts   335
and dampness of the evening; without sentinels set
they sleep the sleep of happiness the whole night through.
And if they reverence the gods who hold the city
and all the holy temples of the captured land,
they, the despoilers, might not be despoiled in turn.   340
Let not their passion overwhelm them; let no lust
seize on these men to violate what they must not.
The run to safety and home is yet to make; they must turn
the pole, and run the backstretch of the double course.
Yet, though the host come home without offence to high   345
gods, even so the anger of these slaughtered men
may never sleep. Oh, let there be no fresh wrong done!

Such are the thoughts you hear from me, a woman merely.
Yet may the best win through, that none may fail to see.
Of all good things to wish this is my dearest choice.   350

Chorus

My lady, no grave man could speak with better grace.
I have listened to the proofs of your tale, and I believe,
and go to make my glad thanksgivings to the gods.
This pleasure is not unworthy of the grief that gave it.

O Zeus our lord and Night beloved,   355
bestower of power and beauty,
you slung above the bastions of Troy
the binding net, that none, neither great
nor young, might outleap
the gigantic toils   360
of enslavement and final disaster.
I gaze in awe on Zeus of the guests
who wrung from Alexander such payment.
He bent the bow with slow care, that neither
the shaft might hurdle the stars, nor fall   365
spent to the earth, short driven.

They have the stroke of Zeus to tell of.
This thing is clear and you may trace it.
He acted as he had decreed. A man thought
the gods deigned not to punish mortals   370
who trampled down the delicacy of things
inviolable. That man was wicked.
The curse on great daring
shines clear; it wrings atonement   375
from those high hearts that drive to evil,
from houses blossoming to pride
and peril. Let there be
wealth without tears; enough for
the wise man who will ask no further.   380
There is not any armor
in gold against perdition
for him who spurns the high altar
of Justice down to the darkness.

Persuasion the persistent overwhelms him,   385
she, strong daughter of designing Ruin.
And every medicine is vain; the sin
smolders not, but burns to evil beauty.
As cheap bronze tortured   390
at the touchstone relapses

to blackness and grime, so this man
tested shows vain
as a child that strives to catch the bird flying
and wins shame that shall bring down his city.   395
No god will hear such a man's entreaty,
but whoso turns to these ways
they strike him down in his wickedness.
This was Paris: he came
to the house of the sons of Atreus,   400
stole the woman away, and shamed
the guest's right of the board shared.

She left among her people the stir and clamor
of shields and of spearheads,   405
the ships to sail and the armor.
She took to Ilium her dowry, death.
She stepped forth lightly between the gates
daring beyond all daring. And the prophets
about the great house wept aloud and spoke:
"Alas, alas for the house and for the champions,   410
alas for the bed signed with their love together.
Here now is silence, scorned, unreproachful.
The agony of his loss is clear before us.
Longing for her who lies beyond the sea
he shall see a phantom queen in his household.   415
Her images in their beauty
are bitterness to her lord now
where in the emptiness of eyes
all passion has faded."

Shining in dreams the sorrowful   420
memories pass; they bring him
vain delight only.
It is vain, to dream and to see splendors,
and the image slipping from the arms' embrace
escapes, not to return again,   425
on wings drifting down the ways of sleep.

Such have the sorrows been in the house by the hearthside;
such have there been, and yet there are worse than these.
In all Hellas, for those who swarmed to the host
the heartbreaking misery   430
shows in the house of each.
Many are they who are touched at the heart by these things.
Those they sent forth they knew;
now, in place of the young men
urns and ashes are carried home   435
to the houses of the fighters.

The god of war, money changer of dead bodies,
held the balance of his spear in the fighting,
and from the corpse-fires at Ilium   440
sent to their dearest the dust
heavy and bitter with tears shed
packing smooth the urns with
ashes that once were men.
They praise them through their tears, how this man   445
knew well the craft of battle, how another
went down splendid in the slaughter:
and all for some strange woman.
Thus they mutter in secrecy,
and the slow anger creeps below their grief   450
at Atreus' sons and their quarrels.
There by the walls of Ilium
the young men in their beauty keep
graves deep in the alien soil
they hated and they conquered.   455

The citizens speak: their voice is dull with hatred.
The curse of the people must be paid for.
There lurks for me in the hooded night
terror of what may be told me.   460
The gods fail not to mark
those who have killed many.
The black Furies stalking the man

fortunate beyond all right
wrench back again the set of his life   465
and drop him to darkness. There among
the ciphers there is no more comfort
in power. And the vaunt of high glory
is bitterness; for God's thunderbolts
crash on the towering mountains.   470
Let me attain no envied wealth,
let me not plunder cities,
neither be taken in turn, and face
life in the power of another.

    (Various members of the Chorus, speaking severally.)

From the beacon's bright message   475
the fleet rumor runs
through the city. If this be real
who knows? Perhaps the gods have sent some lie to us.

Who of us is so childish or so reft of wit
that by the beacon's messages   480
his heart flamed must despond again
when the tale changes in the end?

It is like a woman indeed
to take the rapture before the fact has shown for true.

They believe too easily, are too quick to shift   485
from ground to ground; and swift indeed
the rumor voiced by a woman dies again.

Now we shall understand these torches and their shining,
the beacons, and the interchange of flame and flame.   490
They may be real; yet bright and dreamwise ecstasy
in light's appearance might have charmed our hearts awry.
I see a herald coming from the beach, his brows
shaded with sprigs of olive; and upon his feet
the dust, dry sister of the mire, makes plain to me   495
that he will find a voice, not merely kindle flame
from mountain timber, and make signals from the smoke,

but tell us outright, whether to be happy, or—
but I shrink back from naming the alternative.
That which appeared was good; may yet more good be given.   500

And any man who prays that different things befall
the city, may he reap the crime of his own heart.

(*The Herald enters, and speaks.*)

Soil of my fathers, Argive earth I tread upon,
in daylight of the tenth year I have come back to you.
All my hopes broke but one, and this I have at last.   505
I never could have dared to dream that I might die
in Argos, and be buried in this beloved soil.
Hail to the Argive land and to its sunlight, hail
to its high sovereign, Zeus, and to the Pythian king.
May you no longer shower your arrows on our heads.   510
Beside Scamandrus you were grim; be satisfied
and turn to savior now and healer of our hurts,
my lord Apollo. Gods of the market place assembled,
I greet you all, and my own patron deity
Hermes, beloved herald, in whose right all heralds   515
are sacred; and you heroes that sent forth the host,
propitiously take back all that the spear has left.
O great hall of the kings and house beloved; seats
of sanctity; divinities that face the sun:
if ever before, look now with kind and glowing eyes   520
to greet our king in state after so long a time.
He comes, lord Agamemnon, bearing light in gloom
to you, and to all that are assembled here.
Salute him with good favor, as he well deserves,
the man who has wrecked Ilium with the spade of Zeus   525
vindictive, whereby all their plain has been laid waste.
Gone are their altars, the sacred places of the gods
are gone, and scattered all the seed within the ground.
With such a yoke as this gripped to the neck of Troy
he comes, the king, Atreus' elder son, a man   530

fortunate to be honored far above all men
alive; not Paris nor the city tied to him
can boast he did more than was done him in return.
Guilty of rape and theft, condemned, he lost the prize
captured, and broke to sheer destruction all the house   535
of his fathers, with the very ground whereon it stood.
Twice over the sons of Priam have atoned their sins.

Chorus

Hail and be glad, herald of the Achaean host.

Herald

I am happy; I no longer ask the gods for death.

Chorus

Did passion for your country so strip bare your heart?   540

Herald

So that the tears broke in my eyes, for happiness.

Chorus

You were taken with that sickness, then, that brings delight.

Herald

How? I cannot deal with such words until I understand.

Chorus

Struck with desire of those who loved as much again.

Herald

You mean our country longed for us, as we for home?   545

Chorus

So that I sighed, out of the darkness of my heart.

Herald

Whence came this black thought to afflict the mind with fear?

Chorus

Long since it was my silence kept disaster off.

Herald

But how? There were some you feared when the kings went
away?

Chorus

So much that as you said now, even death were grace.   550

Herald

Well: the end has been good. And in the length of time
part of our fortune you could say held favorable,
but part we cursed again. And who, except the gods,
can live time through forever without any pain?
Were I to tell you of the hard work done, the nights   555
exposed, the cramped sea-quarters, the foul beds—what part
of day's disposal did we not cry out loud?
Ashore, the horror stayed with us and grew. We lay
against the ramparts of our enemies, and from
the sky, and from the ground, the meadow dews came out   560
to soak our clothes and fill our hair with lice. And if
I were to tell of winter time, when all birds died,
the snows of Ida past endurance she sent down,
or summer heat, when in the lazy noon the sea
fell level and asleep under a windless sky—   565
but why live such grief over again? That time is gone
for us, and gone for those who died. Never again
need they rise up, nor care again for anything.
Why must a live man count the numbers of the slain,
why grieve at fortune's wrath that fades to break once more?   570
I call a long farewell to all our unhappiness.
For us, survivors of the Argive armament,
the pleasure wins, pain casts no weight in the opposite scale.
And here, in this sun's shining, we can boast aloud,
whose fame has gone with wings across the land and sea: 575
"Upon a time the Argive host took Troy, and on
the houses of the gods who live in Hellas nailed
the spoils, to be the glory of days long ago."
And they who hear such things shall call this city blest
and the leaders of the host; and high the grace of God   580
shall be exalted, that did this. You have the story.

Chorus

I must give way; your story shows that I was wrong.
Old men are always young enough to learn, with profit.

But Clytaemestra and her house must hear, above
others, this news that makes luxurious my life.   585

(*Clytaemestra comes forward and speaks.*)

I raised my cry of joy, and it was long ago
when the first beacon flare of message came by night
to speak of capture and of Ilium's overthrow.
But there was one who laughed at me, who said: "You trust   590
in beacons so, and you believe that Troy has fallen?
How like a woman, for the heart to lift so light."
Men spoke like that; they thought I wandered in my wits;
yet I made sacrifice, and in the womanish strain
voice after voice caught up the cry along the city   595
to echo in the temples of the gods and bless
and still the fragrant flame that melts the sacrifice.

Why should you tell me then the whole long tale at large
when from my lord himself I shall hear all the story?
But now, how best to speed my preparation to   600
receive my honored lord come home again—what else
is light more sweet for woman to behold than this,
to spread the gates before her husband home from war
and saved by God's hand?—take this message to the king:
Come, and with speed, back to the city that longs for him,   605
and may he find a wife within his house as true
as on the day he left her, watchdog of the house
gentle to him alone, fierce to his enemies,
and such a woman in all her ways as this, who has
not broken the seal upon her in the length of days.   610
With no man else have I known delight, nor any shame
of evil speech, more than I know how to temper bronze.

(*Clytaemestra goes to the back of the stage.*)

Herald

A vaunt like this, so loaded as it is with truth,
it well becomes a highborn lady to proclaim.

Chorus

    Thus has she spoken to you, and well you understand,   615
    words that impress interpreters whose thought is clear.
    But tell me, herald; I would learn of Menelaus,
    that power beloved in this land. Has he survived
    also, and come with you back to his home again?

Herald

    I know no way to lie and make my tale so fair   620
    that friends could reap joy of it for any length of time.

Chorus

    Is there no means to speak us fair, and yet tell the truth?
    It will not hide, when truth and good are torn asunder.

Herald

    He is gone out of the sight of the Achaean host,
    vessel and man alike. I speak no falsehood there.   625

Chorus

    Was it when he had put out from Ilium in your sight,
    or did a storm that struck you both whirl him away?

Herald

    How like a master bowman you have hit the mark
    and in your speech cut a long sorrow to brief stature.

Chorus

    But then the rumor in the host that sailed beside,   630
    was it that he had perished, or might yet be living?

Herald

    No man knows. There is none could tell us that for sure
    except the Sun, from whom this earth has life and increase.

Chorus

    How did this storm, by wrath of the divinities,
    strike on our multitude at sea? How did it end?   635

Herald

    It is not well to stain the blessing of this day
    with speech of evil weight. Such gods are honored apart.

And when the messenger of a shaken host, sad faced,
brings to his city news it prayed never to hear,
this scores one wound upon the body of the people;   640
and that from many houses many men are slain
by the two-lashed whip dear to the War God's hand, this turns
disaster double-bladed, bloodily made two.
The messenger so freighted with a charge of tears
should make his song of triumph at the Furies' door.   645
But, carrying the fair message of our hopes' salvation,
come home to a glad city's hospitality,
how shall I mix my gracious news with foul, and tell
of the storm on the Achaeans by God's anger sent?
For they, of old the deepest enemies, sea and fire,   650
made a conspiracy and gave the oath of hand
to blast in ruin our unhappy Argive army.
At night the sea began to rise in waves of death.
Ship against ship the Thracian stormwind shattered us,
and gored and split, our vessels, swept in violence   655
of storm and whirlwind, beaten by the breaking rain,
drove on in darkness, spun by the wicked shepherd's hand.
But when the sun came up again to light the dawn,
we saw the Aegaean Sea blossoming with dead men,
the men of Achaea, and the wreckage of their ships.   660
For us, and for our ship, some god, no man, by guile
or by entreaty's force prevailing, laid his hand
upon the helm and brought us through with hull unscarred.
Life-giving fortune deigned to take our ship in charge
that neither riding in deep water she took the surf   665
nor drove to shoal and break upon some rocky shore.
But then, delivered from death at sea, in the pale day,
incredulous of our own luck, we shepherded
in our sad thoughts the fresh disaster of the fleet
so pitifully torn and shaken by the storm.   670
Now of these others, if there are any left alive
they speak of us as men who perished, must they not?
Even as we, who fear that they are gone. But may

it all come well in the end. For Menelaus: be sure
if any of them come back that he will be the first.   675
If he is still where some sun's gleam can track him down,
alive and open-eyed, by blessed hand of God
who willed that not yet should his seed be utterly gone,
there is some hope that he will still come home again.
You have heard all; and be sure, you have heard the truth.   680

                                                    (*The Herald goes out.*)

Chorus

  Who is he that named you so
  fatally in every way?
  Could it be some mind unseen
  in divination of your destiny
  shaping to the lips that name   685
  for the bride of spears and blood,
  Helen, which is death? Appropriately
  death of ships, death of men and cities
  from the bower's soft curtained   690
  and secluded luxury she sailed then,
  driven on the giant west wind,
  and armored men in their thousands came,
  huntsmen down the oar blade's fading footprint   695
  to struggle in blood with those
  who by the banks of Simoeis
  beached their hulls where the leaves break.

  And on Ilium in truth
  in the likeness of the name   700
  the sure purpose of the Wrath drove
  marriage with death: for the guest board
  shamed, and Zeus kindly to strangers,
  the vengeance wrought on those men
  who graced in too loud voice the bride-song   705
  fallen to their lot to sing,
  the kinsmen and the brothers.
  And changing its song's measure

the ancient city of Priam   710
chants in high strain of lamentation,
calling Paris him of the fatal marriage;
for it endured its life's end
in desolation and tears
and the piteous blood of its people.   715

Once a man fostered in his house
a lion cub, from the mother's milk
torn, craving the breast given.
In the first steps of its young life   720
mild, it played with children
and delighted the old.
Caught in the arm's cradle
they pampered it like a newborn child,
shining eyed and broken to the hand   725
to stay the stress of its hunger.

But it grew with time, and the lion
in the blood strain came out; it paid
grace to those who had fostered it
in blood and death for the sheep flocks,   730
a grim feast forbidden.
The house reeked with blood run
nor could its people beat down the bane,
the giant murderer's onslaught.
This thing they raised in their house was blessed   735
by God to be priest of destruction.

And that which first came to the city of Ilium,
call it a dream of calm
and the wind dying,
the loveliness and luxury of much gold,   740
the melting shafts of the eyes' glances,
the blossom that breaks the heart with longing.
But she turned in mid-step of her course to make
bitter the consummation,   745

whirling on Priam's people
to blight with her touch and nearness.
Zeus hospitable sent her,
a vengeance to make brides weep.

It has been made long since and grown old among men,   750
this saying: human wealth
grown to fulness of stature
breeds again nor dies without issue.
From high good fortune in the blood   755
blossoms the quenchless agony.
Far from others I hold my own
mind; only the act of evil
breeds others to follow,
young sins in its own likeness.   760
Houses clear in their right are given
children in all loveliness.

But Pride aging is made
in men's dark actions
ripe with the young pride   765
late or soon when the dawn of destiny
comes and birth is given
to the spirit none may fight nor beat down,
sinful Daring; and in those halls
the black visaged Disasters stamped   770
in the likeness of their fathers.

And Righteousness is a shining in
the smoke of mean houses.
Her blessing is on the just man.   775
From high halls starred with gold by reeking hands
she turns back
with eyes that glance away to the simple in heart,
spurning the strength of gold
stamped false with flattery.   780
And all things she steers to fulfilment.

(Agamemnon enters in a chariot, with Cassandra beside
him. The Chorus speaks to him.)

Behold, my king: sacker of Troy's citadel,
own issue of Atreus.
How shall I hail you? How give honor   785
not crossing too high nor yet bending short
of this time's graces?
For many among men are they who set high
the show of honor, yet break justice.
If one be unhappy, all else are fain   790
to grieve with him: yet the teeth of sorrow
come nowise near to the heart's edge.
And in joy likewise they show joy's semblance,
and torture the face to the false smile.
Yet the good shepherd, who knows his flock,   795
the eyes of men cannot lie to him,
that with water of feigned
love seem to smile from the true heart.
But I: when you marshalled this armament
for Helen's sake, I will not hide it,   800
in ugly style you were written in my heart
for steering aslant the mind's course
to bring home by blood
sacrifice and dead men that wild spirit.
But now, in love drawn up from the deep heart,   805
not skimmed at the edge, we hail you.
You have won, your labor is made gladness.
Ask all men: you will learn in time
which of your citizens have been just
in the city's sway, which were reckless.   810

Agamemnon

To Argos first, and to the gods within the land,
I must give due greeting; they have worked with me to bring
me home; they helped me in the vengeance I have wrought
on Priam's city. Not from the lips of men the gods
heard justice, but in one firm cast they laid their votes   815

within the urn of blood that Ilium must die
and all her people; while above the opposite vase
the hand hovered and there was hope, but no vote fell.
The stormclouds of their ruin live; the ash that dies
upon them gushes still in smoke their pride of wealth.   820
For all this we must thank the gods with grace of much
high praise and memory, we who fenced within our toils
of wrath the city; and, because one woman strayed,
the beast of Argos broke them, the fierce young within
the horse, the armored people who marked out their leap   825
against the setting of the Pleiades. A wild
and bloody lion swarmed above the towers of Troy
to glut its hunger lapping at the blood of kings.

This to the gods, a prelude strung to length of words.
But, for the thought you spoke, I heard and I remember   830
and stand behind you. For I say that it is true.
In few men is it part of nature to respect
a friend's prosperity without begrudging him,
as envy's wicked poison settling to the heart
piles up the pain in one sick with unhappiness,   835
who, staggered under sufferings that are all his own,
winces again to the vision of a neighbor's bliss.
And I can speak, for I have seen, I know it well,
this mirror of companionship, this shadow's ghost,
these men who seemed my friends in all sincerity.   840
One man of them all, Odysseus, he who sailed unwilling,
once yoked to me carried his harness, nor went slack.
Dead though he be or living, I can say it still.

Now in the business of the city and the gods
we must ordain full conclave of all citizens   845
and take our counsel. We shall see what element
is strong, and plan that it shall keep its virtue still.
But that which must be healed—we must use medicine,
or burn, or amputate, with kind intention, take
all means at hand that might beat down corruption's pain.   850

So to the King's house and the home about the hearth
I take my way, with greeting to the gods within
who sent me forth, and who have brought me home once more.
My prize was conquest; may it never fail again.

(*Clytaemestra comes forward and speaks.*)

Grave gentlemen of Argolis assembled here,   855
I take no shame to speak aloud before you all
the love I bear my husband. In the lapse of time
modesty fades; it is human.

What I tell you now
I learned not from another; this is my own sad life
all the long years this man was gone at Ilium.   860
It is evil and a thing of terror when a wife
sits in the house forlorn with no man by, and hears
rumors that like a fever die to break again,
and men come in with news of fear, and on their heels
another messenger, with worse news to cry aloud   865
here in this house. Had Agamemnon taken all
the wounds the tale whereof was carried home to me,
he had been cut full of gashes like a fishing net.
If he had died each time that rumor told his death,
he must have been some triple-bodied Geryon   870
back from the dead with threefold cloak of earth upon
his body, and killed once for every shape assumed.
Because such tales broke out forever on my rest,
many a time they cut me down and freed my throat   875
from the noose overslung where I had caught it fast.
And therefore is your son, in whom my love and yours
are sealed and pledged, not here to stand with us today,
Orestes. It were right; yet do not be amazed.
Strophius of Phocis, comrade in arms and faithful friend   880
to you, is keeping him. He spoke to me of peril
on two counts; of your danger under Ilium,
and here, of revolution and the clamorous people
who might cast down the council—since it lies in men's

nature to trample on the fighter already down.   885
Such my excuse to you, and without subterfuge.

For me: the rippling springs that were my tears have dried
utterly up, nor left one drop within. I keep
the pain upon my eyes where late at night I wept
over the beacons long ago set for your sake,   890
untended left forever. In the midst of dreams
the whisper that a gnat's thin wings could winnow broke
my sleep apart. I thought I saw you suffer wounds
more than the time that slept with me could ever hold.

Now all my suffering is past, with griefless heart   895
I hail this man, the watchdog of the fold and hall;
the stay that keeps the ship alive; the post to grip
groundward the towering roof; a father's single child;
land seen by sailors after all their hope was gone;
splendor of daybreak shining from the night of storm;   900
the running spring a parched wayfarer strays upon.
Oh, it is sweet to escape from all necessity!

Such is my greeting to him, that he well deserves.
Let none bear malice; for the harm that went before
I took, and it was great.
                                   Now, my beloved one,   905
step from your chariot; yet let not your foot, my lord,
sacker of Ilium, touch the earth. My maidens there!
Why this delay? Your task has been appointed you,
to strew the ground before his feet with tapestries.
Let there spring up into the house he never hoped   910
to see, where Justice leads him in, a crimson path.

In all things else, my heart's unsleeping care shall act
with the gods' aid to set aright what fate ordained.

> (*Clytaemestra's handmaidens spread a bright carpet*
> *between the chariot and the door.*)

Agamemnon

Daughter of Leda, you who kept my house for me,
there is one way your welcome matched my absence well.   915

You strained it to great length. Yet properly to praise
me thus belongs by right to other lips, not yours.
And all this—do not try in woman's ways to make
me delicate, nor, as if I were some Asiatic
bow down to earth and with wide mouth cry out to me,   920
nor cross my path with jealousy by strewing the ground
with robes. Such state becomes the gods, and none beside.
I am a mortal, a man; I cannot trample upon
these tinted splendors without fear thrown in my path.
I tell you, as a man, not god, to reverence me.   925
Discordant is the murmur at such treading down
of lovely things; while God's most lordly gift to man
is decency of mind. Call that man only blest
who has in sweet tranquillity brought his life to close.
If I could only act as such, my hope is good.   930

Clytaemestra

Yet tell me this one thing, and do not cross my will.

Agamemnon

My will is mine. I shall not make it soft for you.

Clytaemestra

It was in fear surely that you vowed this course to God.

Agamemnon

No man has spoken knowing better what he said.

Clytaemestra

If Priam had won as you have, what would he have done?   935

Agamemnon

I well believe he might have walked on tapestries.

Clytaemestra

Be not ashamed before the bitterness of men.

Agamemnon

The people murmur, and their voice is great in strength.

Clytaemestra

Yet he who goes unenvied shall not be admired.

Agamemnon

Surely this lust for conflict is not womanlike?   940

Clytaemestra

Yet for the mighty even to give way is grace.

Agamemnon

Does such a victory as this mean so much to you?

Clytaemestra

Oh yield! The power is yours. Give way of your free will.

Agamemnon

Since you must have it—here, let someone with all speed
take off these sandals, slaves for my feet to tread upon.   945
And as I crush these garments stained from the rich sea
let no god's eyes of hatred strike me from afar.
Great the extravagance, and great the shame I feel
to spoil such treasure and such silver's worth of webs.

So much for all this. Take this stranger girl within   950
now, and be kind. The conqueror who uses softly
his power, is watched from far in the kind eyes of God,
and this slave's yoke is one no man will wear from choice.
Gift of the host to me, and flower exquisite
from all my many treasures, she attends me here.   955

Now since my will was bent to listen to you in this
my feet crush purple as I pass within the hall.

Clytaemestra

The sea is there, and who shall drain its yield? It breeds
precious as silver, ever of itself renewed,
the purple ooze wherein our garments shall be dipped.   960
And by God's grace this house keeps full sufficiency
of all. Poverty is a thing beyond its thought.
I could have vowed to trample many splendors down

Clytaemestra

You try me out as if I were a woman and vain;
but my heart is not fluttered as I speak before you.
You know it. You can praise or blame me as you wish;
it is all one to me. That man is Agamemnon,
my husband; he is dead; the work of this right hand   1405
that struck in strength of righteousness. And that is that.

Chorus

Woman, what evil thing planted upon the earth
or dragged from the running salt sea could you have tasted now
to wear such brutality and walk in the people's hate?
You have cast away, you have cut away. You shall go homeless
    now,   1410
crushed with men's bitterness.

Clytaemestra

Now it is I you doom to be cast out from my city
with men's hate heaped and curses roaring in my ears.
Yet look upon this dead man; you would not cross him once
when with no thought more than as if a beast had died,   1415
when his ranged pastures swarmed with the deep fleece of flocks,
he slaughtered like a victim his own child, my pain
grown into love, to charm away the winds of Thrace.
Were you not bound to hunt him then clear of this soil
for the guilt stained upon him? Yet you hear what I   1420
have done, and lo, you are a stern judge. But I say to you:
go on and threaten me, but know that I am ready,
if fairly you can beat me down beneath your hand,
for you to rule; but if the god grant otherwise,
you shall be taught—too late, for sure—to keep your place.   1425

Chorus

Great your design, your speech is a clamor of pride.
Swung to the red act drives the fury within your brain
signed clear in the splash of blood over your eyes.
Yet to come is stroke given for stroke
vengeless, forlorn of friends.   1430

Clytaemestra

Now hear you this, the right behind my sacrament:
By my child's Justice driven to fulfilment, by
her Wrath and Fury, to whom I sacrificed this man,
the hope that walks my chambers is not traced with fear
while yet Aegisthus makes the fire shine on my hearth,   1435
my good friend, now as always, who shall be for us
the shield of our defiance, no weak thing; while he,
this other, is fallen, stained with this woman you behold,
plaything of all the golden girls at Ilium;
and here lies she, the captive of his spear, who saw   1440
wonders, who shared his bed, the wise in revelations
and loving mistress, who yet knew the feel as well
of the men's rowing benches. Their reward is not
unworthy. He lies there; and she who swanlike cried
aloud her lyric mortal lamentation out   1445
is laid against his fond heart, and to me has given
a delicate excitement to my bed's delight.

Chorus

O that in speed, without pain
and the slow bed of sickness
death could come to us now, death that forever   1450
carries sleep without ending, now that our lord is down,
our shield, kindest of men,
who for a woman's grace suffered so much,
struck down at last by a woman.

Alas, Helen, wild heart   1455
for the multitudes, for the thousand lives
you killed under Troy's shadow,
you alone, to shine in man's memory
as blood flower never to be washed out. Surely a demon then   1460
of death walked in the house, men's agony.

Clytaemestra

No, be not so heavy, nor yet draw down
in prayer death's ending,

neither turn all wrath against Helen
for men dead, that she alone killed   1465
all those Danaan lives, to work
the grief that is past all healing.

Chorus

Divinity that kneel on this house and the two
strains of the blood of Tantalus,
in the hands and hearts of women you steer   1470
the strength tearing my heart.
Standing above the corpse, obscene
as some carrion crow she sings
the crippled song and is proud.

Clytaemestra

Thus have you set the speech of your lips   1475
straight, calling by name
the spirit thrice glutted that lives in this race.
From him deep in the nerve is given
the love and the blood drunk, that before
the old wound dries, it bleeds again.   1480

Chorus

Surely it is a huge
and heavy spirit bending the house you cry;
alas, the bitter glory
of a doom that shall never be done with;
and all through Zeus, Zeus,   1485
first cause, prime mover.
For what thing without Zeus is done among mortals?
What here is without God's blessing?

O king, my king
how shall I weep for you?   1490
What can I say out of my heart of pity?
Caught in this spider's web you lie,
Your life gasped out in indecent death,
struck prone to this shameful bed

by your lady's hand of treachery 1495
and the stroke twin edged of the iron.

Clytaemestra

Can you claim I have done this?
Speak of me never
more as the wife of Agamemnon.
In the shadow of this corpse's queen 1500
the old stark avenger
of Atreus for his revel of hate
struck down this man,
last blood for the slaughtered children.

Chorus

What man shall testify 1505
your hands are clean of this murder?
How? How? Yet from his father's blood
might swarm some fiend to guide you.
The black ruin that shoulders
through the streaming blood of brothers 1510
strides at last where he shall win requital
for the children who were eaten.

O king, my king
how shall I weep for you?
What can I say out of my heart of pity? 1515
Caught in this spider's web you lie,
your life gasped out in indecent death,
struck prone to this shameful bed
by your lady's hand of treachery
and the stroke twin edged of the iron. 1520

Clytaemestra

No shame, I think, in the death given
this man. And did he not
first of all in this house wreak death
by treachery?
The flower of this man's love and mine, 1525

Iphigeneia of the tears
he dealt with even as he has suffered.
Let his speech in death's house be not loud.
With the sword he struck,
with the sword he paid for his own act.

Chorus

My thoughts are swept away and I go bewildered.   1530
Where shall I turn the brain's
activity in speed when the house is falling?
There is fear in the beat of the blood rain breaking
wall and tower. The drops come thicker.
Still fate grinds on yet more stones the blade   1535
for more acts of terror.

Earth, my earth, why did you not fold me under
before ever I saw this man lie dead
fenced by the tub in silver?   1540
Who shall bury him? Who shall mourn him?
Shall you dare this who have killed
your lord? Make lamentation,
render the graceless grace to his soul   1545
for huge things done in wickedness?
Who over this great man's grave shall lay
the blessing of tears
worked soberly from a true heart?   1550

Clytaemestra

Not for you to speak of such tendance.
Through us he fell,
by us he died; we shall bury.
There will be no tears in this house for him.
It must be Iphigeneia   1555
his child, who else,
shall greet her father by the whirling stream
and the ferry of tears
to close him in her arms and kiss him.

Chorus

Here is anger for anger. Between them 1560
who shall judge lightly?
The spoiler is robbed; he killed, he has paid.
The truth stands ever beside God's throne
eternal: he who has wrought shall pay; that is law.
Then who shall tear the curse from their blood? 1565
The seed is stiffened to ruin.

Clytaemestra

You see truth in the future
at last. Yet I wish
to seal my oath with the Spirit
in the house: I will endure all things as they stand 1570
now, hard though it be. Hereafter
let him go forth to make bleed with death
and guilt the houses of others.
I will take some small
measure of our riches, and be content
that I swept from these halls 1575
the murder, the sin, and the fury.

(*Aegisthus enters, followed at a little distance by his
armed bodyguard.*)

Aegisthus

O splendor and exaltation of this day of doom!
Now I can say once more that the high gods look down
on mortal crimes to vindicate the right at last,
now that I see this man—sweet sight—before me here 1580
sprawled in the tangling nets of fury, to atone
the calculated evil of his father's hand.
For Atreus, this man's father, King of Argolis—
I tell you the clear story—drove my father forth,
Thyestes, his own brother, who had challenged him 1585
in his king's right—forth from his city and his home.
Yet sad Thyestes came again to supplicate
the hearth, and win some grace, in that he was not slain

nor soiled the doorstone of his fathers with blood spilled.
Not his own blood. But Atreus, this man's godless sire,   1590
angrily hospitable set a feast for him,
in seeming a glad day of fresh meat slain and good
cheer; then served my father his own children's flesh
to feed on. For he carved away the extremities,
hands, feet, and cut the flesh apart, and covered them   1595
served in a dish to my father at his table apart,
who with no thought for the featureless meal before him ate
that ghastly food whose curse works now before your eyes.
But when he knew the terrible thing that he had done,
he spat the dead meat from him with a cry, and reeled   1600
spurning the table back to heel with strength the curse:
"Thus crash in ruin all the seed of Pleisthenes."
Out of such acts you see this dead man stricken here,
and it was I, in my right, who wrought this murder, I
third born to my unhappy father, and with him   1605
driven, a helpless baby in arms, to banishment.
Yet I grew up, and justice brought me home again,
till from afar I laid my hands upon this man,
since it was I who pieced together the fell plot.
Now I can die in honor again, if die I must,   1610
having seen him caught in the cords of his just punishment.

Chorus

Aegisthus, this strong vaunting in distress is vile,
You claim that you deliberately killed the king,
you, and you only, wrought the pity of this death.
I tell you then: There shall be no escape, your head   1615
shall face the stones of anger from the people's hands.

Aegisthus

So loud from you, stooped to the meanest rowing bench
with the ship's masters lordly on the deck above?
You are old men; well, you shall learn how hard it is
at your age, to be taught how to behave yourselves.   1620
But there are chains, there is starvation with its pain,

excellent teachers of good manners to old men,
wise surgeons and exemplars. Look! Can you not see it?
Lash not at the goads for fear you hit them, and be hurt.

Chorus

So then you, like a woman, waited the war out   1625
here in the house, shaming the master's bed with lust,
and planned against the lord of war this treacherous death?

Aegisthus

It is just such words as these will make you cry in pain.
Not yours the lips of Orpheus, no, quite otherwise,
whose voice of rapture dragged all creatures in his train.   1630
You shall be dragged, for baby whimperings sobbed out
in rage. Once broken, you will be easier to deal with.

Chorus

How shall you be lord of the men of Argos, you
who planned the murder of this man, yet could not dare
to act it out, and cut him down with your own hand?   1635

Aegisthus

No, clearly the deception was the woman's part,
and I was suspect, that had hated him so long.
Still with his money I shall endeavor to control
the citizens. The mutinous man shall feel the yoke
drag at his neck, no cornfed racing colt that runs   1640
free traced; but hunger, grim companion of the dark
dungeon shall see him broken to the hand at last.

Chorus

But why, why then, you coward, could you not have slain
your man yourself? Why must it be his wife who killed,
to curse the country and the gods within the ground?   1645
Oh, can Orestes live, be somewhere in sunlight still?
Shall fate grown gracious ever bring him back again
in strength of hand to overwhelm these murderers?

Aegisthus

You shall learn then, since you stick to stubbornness of mouth
and hand.
Up now from your cover, my henchmen: here is work for you
to do.   1650

Chorus

Look, they come! Let every man clap fist upon his hilted sword.

Aegisthus

I too am sword-handed against you; I am not afraid of death.

Chorus

Death you said and death it shall be; we take up the word of
fate.

Clytaemestra

No, my dearest, dearest of all men, we have done enough. No
more
violence. Here is a monstrous harvest and a bitter reaping time.   1655
There is pain enough already. Let us not be bloody now.
Honored gentlemen of Argos, go to your homes now and give
way
to the stress of fate and season. We could not do otherwise
than we did. If this is the end of suffering, we can be content
broken as we are by the brute heel of angry destiny.   1660
Thus a woman speaks among you. Shall men deign to understand?

Aegisthus

Yes, but think of these foolish lips that blossom into leering gibes,
think of the taunts they spit against me daring destiny and power,
sober opinion lost in insults hurled against my majesty.

Chorus

It was never the Argive way to grovel at a vile man's feet.   1665

Aegisthus

I shall not forget this; in the days to come I shall be there.

Chorus

Nevermore, if God's hand guiding brings Orestes home again.

Aegisthus

Exiles feed on empty dreams of hope. I know it. I was one.

Chorus

Have your way, gorge and grow fat, soil justice, while the power is yours.

Aegisthus

You shall pay, make no mistake, for this misguided insolence.   1670

Chorus

Crow and strut, brave cockerel by your hen; you have no threats to fear.

Clytaemestra

These are howls of impotent rage; forget them, dearest; you and I

have the power; we two shall bring good order to our house at least.

(*They enter the house. The doors close. All persons leave the stage.*)

THE LIBATION BEARERS

CHARACTERS

Orestes, son of Agamemnon and Clytaemestra

Pylades, his friend

Electra, his sister

Chorus, of foreign serving-women

A servant (doorkeeper)

Clytaemestra, now wife of Aegisthus, queen of Argos

Cilissa, the nurse

Aegisthus, now king of Argos

A follower of Aegisthus

Various attendants of Orestes, Clytaemestra, Aegisthus (silent parts)

THE LIBATION BEARERS

SCENE: *Argos. The first part of the play (1–651) takes place at the tomb of Agamemnon: the last part (652 to the end) before the door of Clytaemestra's palace. No mechanical change of scene is necessary. The altar or tomb of Agamemnon should be well down stage. The door to the house should be in the center, back.*

(*Enter, as travelers, Orestes and Pylades.*)

Orestes

Hermes, lord of the dead, who watch over the powers
of my fathers, be my savior and stand by my claim.
Here is my own soil that I walk. I have come home;
and by this mounded gravebank I invoke my sire
to hear, to listen.   5
Here is a lock of hair for Inachus, who made
me grow to manhood. Here a strand to mark my grief.
I was not by, my father, to mourn for your death
nor stretched my hand out when they took your corpse away.

(*The chorus, with Electra, enter from the side.*)

But what can this mean that I see, this group that comes   10
of women veiled in dignities of black? At what
sudden occurrence can I guess? Is this some new
wound struck into our house? I think they bring these urns
to pour, in my father's honor, to appease the powers
below. Can I be right? Surely, I think I see   15
Electra, my own sister, walk in bitter show
of mourning. Zeus, Zeus, grant me vengeance for my father's
murder. Stand and fight beside me, of your grace.

Pylades, stand we out of their way. So may I learn
the meaning of these women; what their prayer would ask.   20

Chorus

I came in haste out of the house
to carry libations, hurt by the hard stroke of hands.

My cheek shows bright, ripped in the bloody furrows
of nails gashing the skin.   25
This is my life: to feed the heart on hard-drawn breath.
And in my grief, with splitting weft
of ragtorn linen across my heart's
brave show of robes
came sound of my hands' strokes   30
in sorrows whence smiles are fled.

Terror, the dream diviner of
this house, belled clear, shuddered the skin, blew wrath
from sleep, a cry in night's obscure watches,
a voice of fear deep in the house,   35
dropping deadweight in women's inner chambers.
And they who read the dream meanings
and spoke under guarantee of God
told how under earth
dead men held a grudge still   40
and smoldered at their murderers.

On such grace without grace, evil's turning aside
(Earth, Earth, kind mother!)
bent, the godless woman
sends me forth. But terror   45
is on me for this word let fall.
What can wash off the blood once spilled upon the ground?
O hearth soaked in sorrow,
o wreckage of a fallen house.
Sunless and where men fear to walk   50
the mists huddle upon this house
where the high lords have perished.

The pride not to be warred with, fought with, not to be beaten
    down
of old, sounded in all men's   55
ears, in all hearts sounded,
has shrunk away. A man
goes in fear. High fortune,

this in man's eyes is god and more than god is this.   60
But, as a beam balances, so
sudden disasters wait, to strike
some in the brightness, some in gloom
of half dark in their elder time.
Desperate night holds others.   65

Through too much glut of blood drunk by our fostering ground
the vengeful gore is caked and hard, will not drain through.
The deep-run ruin carries away
the man of guilt. Swarming infection boils within.   70

For one who handles the bridal close, there is no cure.
All the world's waters running in a single drift
may try to wash blood from the hand
of the stained man; they only bring new blood guilt on.   75

But as for me: gods have forced on my city
resisted fate. From our fathers' houses
they led us here, to take the lot of slaves.
And mine it is to wrench my will, and consent
to their commands, right or wrong,   80
to beat down my edged hate.
And yet under veils I weep
the vanities that have killed
my lord; and freeze with sorrow in the secret heart.

Electra

Attendant women, who order our house, since you
are with me in this supplication and escort   85
me here, be also my advisers in this rite.
What shall I say, as I pour out these outpourings
of sorrow? How say the good word, how make my prayer
to my father? Shall I say I bring it to the man
beloved, from a loving wife, and mean my mother? I   90
have not the daring to say this, nor know what else
to say, as I pour this liquid on my father's tomb.
Shall I say this sentence, regular in human use:

"Grant good return to those who send to you these flowers
of honor: gifts to match the . . . evil they have done." 95

Or, quiet and dishonored, as my father died
shall I pour out this offering for the ground to drink,
and go, like one who empties garbage out of doors,
and turn my eyes, and throw the vessel far away.

Dear friends, in this deliberation stay with me. 100
We hold a common hatred in this house. Do not
for fear of any, hide your thought inside your heart.
The day of destiny waits for the free man as well
as for the man enslaved beneath an alien hand.
If you know any better course than mine, tell me. 105

Chorus

In reverence for your father's tomb as if it were
an altar, I will speak my heart's thought, as you ask.

Electra

Tell me then, please, as you respect my father's grave.

Chorus

Say words of grace for those of good will, as you pour.

Electra

Whom of those closest to me can I call my friend? 110

Chorus

Yourself first; all who hate Aegisthus after that.

Electra

You mean these prayers shall be for you, and for myself?

Chorus

You see it now; but it is you whose thought this is.

Electra

Is there some other we should bring in on our side?

Chorus

Remember Orestes, though he wanders far away. 115

Electra

That was well spoken; you did well reminding me.

Chorus

Remember, too, the murderers, and against them . . .

Electra

What shall I say? Guide and instruct my ignorance.

Chorus

Invoke the coming of some man, or more than man.

Electra

To come to judge them, or to give them punishment?   120

Chorus

Say simply: "one to kill them, for the life they took."

Electra

I can ask this, and not be wrong in the gods' eyes?

Chorus

May you not hurt your enemy, when he struck first?

Electra

Almighty herald of the world above, the world
below: Hermes, lord of the dead, help me; announce
my prayers to the charmed spirits underground, who watch   125
over my father's house, that they may hear. Tell Earth
herself, who brings all things to birth, who gives them strength,
then gathers their big yield into herself at last.
I myself pour these lustral waters to the dead,
and speak, and call upon my father: Pity me;   130
pity your own Orestes. How shall we be lords
in our house? We have been sold, and go as wanderers
because our mother bought herself, for us, a man,
Aegisthus, he who helped her hand to cut you down.
Now I am what a slave is, and Orestes lives   135
outcast from his great properties, while they go proud
in the high style and luxury of what you worked

to win. By some good fortune let Orestes come
back home. Such is my prayer, my father. Hear me; hear.
And for myself, grant that I be more temperate   140
of heart than my mother; that I act with purer hand.

Such are my prayers for us; but for our enemies,
father, I pray that your avenger come, that they
who killed you shall be killed in turn, as they deserve.
Between my prayer for good and prayer for good I set   145
this prayer for evil; and I speak it against Them.
For us, bring blessings up into the world. Let Earth
and conquering Justice, and all gods beside, give aid.

Such are my prayers; and over them I pour these drink
offerings. Yours the strain now, yours to make them flower   150
with mourning song, and incantation for the dead.

Chorus

Let the tear fall, that clashes as it dies
as died our fallen lord;
die on this mound that fences good from evil,
washing away the death stain accursed   155
of drink offerings shed. Hear me, oh hear, my lord,
majesty hear me from your dark heart; oh hear.
Let one come, in strength
of spear, some man at arms who will set free the house   160
holding the Scythian bow backbent in his hands,
a barbarous god of war spattering arrows
or closing to slash, with sword hilted fast to his hand.

Electra

Father, the earth has drunk my offerings poured to you.
Something has happened here, my women. Help me now.   165

Chorus

Speak, if you will. My heart is in a dance of fear.

Electra

Someone has cut a strand of hair and laid it on
the tomb.

Chorus

What man? Or was it some deep-waisted girl?

Electra

There is a mark, which makes it plain for any to guess.   170

Chorus

Explain, and let your youth instruct my elder age.

Electra

No one could have cut off this strand, except myself.

Chorus

Those others, whom it would have become, are full of hate.

Electra

Yet here it is, and for appearance matches well . . .

Chorus

With whose hair? Tell me. This is what I long to know. . . .   175

Electra

With my own hair. It is almost exactly like.

Chorus

Can it then be a secret gift from Orestes?

Electra

It seems that it must be nobody's hair but his.

Chorus

Did Orestes dare to come back here? How could this be?

Electra

He sent this severed strand, to do my father grace.   180

Chorus

It will not stop my tears if you are right. You mean
that he can never again set foot upon this land.

Electra

The bitter wash has surged upon my heart as well.
I am struck through, as by the cross-stab of a sword,

and from my eyes the thirsty and unguarded drops   185
burst in a storm of tears like winter rain, as I
look on this strand of hair. How could I think some other
man, some burgess, could ever go grand in hair like this?
She never could have cut it, she who murdered him
and is my mother, but no mother in her heart   190
which has assumed God's hate and hates her children. No.
And yet, how can I say in open outright confidence
this is a treasured token from the best beloved
of men to me, Orestes? Does hope fawn on me?
Ah
I wish it had the kind voice of a messenger   195
so that my mind would not be torn in two, I not
shaken, but it could tell me plain to throw this strand
away as vile, if it was cut from a hated head,
or like a brother could have mourned with me, and been
a treasured splendor for my father, and his grave.   200

The gods know, and we call upon the gods; they know
how we are spun in circles like seafarers, in
what storms. But if we are to win, and our ship live,
from one small seed could burgeon an enormous tree.

But see, here is another sign. Footprints are here.   205
The feet that made them are alike, and look like mine.
There are two sets of footprints: of the man who gave
his hair, and one who shared the road with him. I step
where he has stepped, and heelmarks, and the space between
his heel and toe are like the prints I make. Oh, this   210
is torment, and my wits are going.

(Orestes comes from his place of concealment.)

Orestes

Pray for what is to come, and tell the gods that they
have brought your former prayers to pass. Pray for success.

Electra

Upon what ground? What have I won yet from the gods?

Orestes

You have come in sight of all you long since prayed to see.   215

Electra

How did you know what man was subject of my prayer?

Orestes

I know about Orestes, how he stirred your heart.

Electra

Yes; but how am I given an answer to my prayers?

Orestes

Look at me. Look for no one closer to you than I.

Electra

Is this some net of treachery, friend, you catch me in?   220

Orestes

Then I must be contriving plots against myself.

Electra

It is your pleasure to laugh at my unhappiness.

Orestes

I only mock my own then, if I laugh at you.

Electra

Are you really Orestes? Can I call you by that name?

Orestes

You see my actual self and are slow to learn. And yet   225
you saw this strand of hair I cut in sign of grief
and shuddered with excitement, for you thought you saw
me, and again when you were measuring my tracks.
Now lay the severed strand against where it was cut
and see how well your brother's hair matches my head.   230
Look at this piece of weaving, the work of your hand
with its blade strokes and figured design of beasts. No, no,
control yourself, and do not lose your head for joy.
I know those nearest to us hate us bitterly.

Electra

 O dearest, treasured darling of my father's house,   235
 hope of the seed of our salvation, wept for, trust
 your strength of hand, and win your father's house again.
 O bright beloved presence, you bring back four lives
 to me. To call you father is constraint of fact,
 and all the love I could have borne my mother turns   240
 your way, while she is loathed as she deserves; my love
 for a pitilessly slaughtered sister turns to you.
 And now you were my steadfast brother after all.
 You alone bring me honor; but let Force, and Right,
 and Zeus almighty, third with them, be on your side.   245

Orestes

 Zeus, Zeus, direct all that we try to do. Behold
 the orphaned children of the eagle-father, now
 that he has died entangled in the binding coils
 of the deadly viper, and the young he left behind
 are worn with hunger of starvation, not full grown   250
 to bring their shelter slain food, as their father did.
 I, with my sister, whom I name, Electra here,
 stand in your sight, children whose father is lost. We both
 are driven from the house that should be ours. If you
 destroy these fledgelings of a father who gave you   255
 sacrifice and high honor, from what hand like his
 shall you be given the sacred feast which is your right?
 Destroy the eagle's brood, and you have no more means
 to send your signs to mortals for their strong belief;
 nor, if the stump rot through on this baronial tree,   260
 shall it sustain your altars on sacrificial days.
 Safe keep it: from a little thing you can raise up
 a house to grandeur, though it now seem overthrown.

Chorus

 O children, silence! Saviors of your father's house,
 be silent, children. Otherwise someone may hear   265
 and for mere love of gossip carry news of all

you do, to those in power, to those I long to see
some day as corpses in the leaking pitch and flame.

Orestes

    The big strength of Apollo's oracle will not
forsake me. For he charged me to win through this hazard,   270
with divination of much, and speech articulate,
the winters of disaster under the warm heart
were I to fail against my father's murderers;
told me to cut them down in their own fashion, turn
to the bull's fury in the loss of my estates.   275
He said that else I must myself pay penalty
with my own life, and suffer much sad punishment;
spoke of the angers that come out of the ground from those
beneath who turn against men; spoke of sicknesses,
ulcers that ride upon the flesh, and cling, and with   280
wild teeth eat away the natural tissue, how on this
disease shall grow in turn a leprous fur. He spoke
of other ways again by which the avengers might
attack, brought to fulfilment from my father's blood.
For the dark arrow of the dead men underground   285
from those within my blood who fell and turn to call
upon me; madness and empty terror in the night
on one who sees clear and whose eyes move in the dark,
must tear him loose and shake him until, with all his bulk
degraded by the bronze-loaded lash, he lose his city.   290
And such as he can have no share in the communal bowl
allowed them, no cup filled for friends to drink. The wrath
of the father comes unseen on them to drive them back
from altars. None can take them in nor shelter them.
Dishonored and unloved by all the man must die   295
at last, shrunken and wasted away in painful death.

    Shall I not trust such oracles as this? Or if
I do not trust them, here is work that must be done.
Here numerous desires converge to drive me on:
the god's urgency and my father's passion, and   300

with these the loss of my estates wears hard on me;
the thought that these my citizens, most high renowned
of men, who toppled Troy in show of courage, must
go subject to this brace of women; since his heart
is female; or, if it be not, that soon will show.   305

Chorus

    Almighty Destinies, by the will
of Zeus let these things
be done, in the turning of Justice.
For the word of hatred spoken, let hate
be a word fulfilled. The spirit of Right   310
cries out aloud and extracts atonement
due: blood stroke for the stroke of blood
shall be paid. Who acts, shall endure. So speaks
the voice of the age-old wisdom.

Orestes

    Father, o my dread father, what thing   315
can I say, can I accomplish
from this far place where I stand, to mark
and reach you there in your chamber
with light that will match your dark?
Yet it is called an action   320
of grace to mourn in style for the house,
once great, of the sons of Atreus.

Chorus

    Child, when the fire burns
and tears with teeth at the dead man
it can not wear out the heart of will.   325
He shows his wrath in the after-
days. One dies, and is dirged.
Light falls on the man who killed him.
He is hunted down by the deathsong
for sires slain and for fathers,   330
disturbed, and stern, and enormous.

Electra

    Hear me, my father; hear in turn
    all the tears of my sorrows.
    Two children stand at your tomb to sing
    the burden of your death chant.   335
    Your grave is shelter to suppliants,
    shelter to the outdriven.
    What here is good; what escape from grief?
    Can we outwrestle disaster?

Chorus

    Yet from such as this the god, if he will,   340
    can work out strains that are fairer.
    For dirges chanted over the grave
    the winner's song in the lordly house;
    bring home to new arms the beloved.

Orestes

    If only at Ilium,   345
    father, and by some Lycian's hands
    you had gone down at the spear's stroke,
    you would have left high fame in your house,
    in the going forth of your children
    eyes' admiration;   350
    founded the deep piled bank of earth
    for grave by the doubled water
    with light lift for your household;

Chorus

    loved then by those he loved
    down there beneath the ground   355
    who died as heroes, he would have held
    state, and a lord's majesty,
    vassal only to those most great,
    the Kings of the under darkness.
    For he was King on earth when he lived   360
    over those whose hands held power of life
    and death, and the staff of authority.

Electra

No, but not under Troy's
ramparts, father, should you have died,
nor, with the rest of the spearstruck hordes   365
have found your grave by Scamandrus' crossing.
Sooner, his murderers
should have been killed, as he was,
by those they loved, and have found their death,
and men remote from this outrage   370
had heard the distant story.

Chorus

Child, child, you are dreaming, since dreaming is a light
pastime, of fortune more golden than gold
or the Blessed Ones north of the North Wind.
But the stroke of the twofold lash is pounding   375
close, and powers gather under ground
to give aid. The hands of those who are lords
are unclean, and these are accursed.
Power grows on the side of the children.

Orestes

This cry has come to your ear   380
like a deep driven arrow.
Zeus, Zeus, force up from below
ground the delayed destruction
on the hard heart and the daring
hand, for the right of our fathers.   385

Chorus

May I claim right to close the deathsong
chanted in glory across
the man speared and the woman
dying. Why darken what deep within me forever
flitters? Long since against the heart's   390
stem a bitter wind has blown
thin anger and burdened hatred.

Electra

> May Zeus, from all shoulder's strength,
> pound down his fist upon them,   395
> ohay, smash their heads.
> Let the land once more believe.
> There has been wrong done. I ask for right.
> Hear me, Earth. Hear me, grandeurs of Darkness.

Chorus

> It is but law that when the red drops have been spilled   400
> upon the ground they cry aloud for fresh
> blood. For the death act calls out on Fury
> to bring out of those who were slain before
> new ruin on ruin accomplished.

Orestes

> Hear me, you lordships of the world below.   405
> Behold in assembled power, curses come from the dead,
> behold the last of the sons of Atreus, foundering
> lost, without future, cast
> from house and right. O god, where shall we turn?

Chorus

> The heart jumped in me once again   410
> to hear this unhappy prayer.
> I was disconsolate then
> and the deep heart within
> darkened to hear you speak it.
> But when strength came back hope lifted   415
> me again, and the sorrow
> was gone and the light was on me.

Electra

> Of what thing can we speak, and strike more close,
> than of the sorrows they who bore us have given?
> So let her fawn if she likes. It softens not.   420
> For we are bloody like the wolf
> and savage born from the savage mother.

Chorus

> I struck my breast in the stroke-style of the Arian,
> the Cissian mourning woman,
> and the hail-beat of the drifting fists was there to see   425
> as the rising pace went in a pattern of blows
> downward and upward until the crashing strokes
> played on my hammered, my all-stricken head.

Electra

> O cruel, cruel
> all daring mother, in cruel processional   430
> with all his citizens gone,
> with all sorrow for him forgotten
> you dared bury your unbewept lord.

Orestes

> O all unworthy of him, that you tell me.
> Shall she not pay for this dishonor   435
> for all the immortals,
> for all my own hands can do?
> Let me but take her life and die for it.

Chorus

> Know then, they hobbled him beneath the armpits,
> with his own hands. She wrought so, in his burial   440
> to make his death a burden
> beyond your strength to carry.
> The mutilation of your father. Hear it.

Electra

> You tell of how my father was murdered. Meanwhile I   445
> stood apart, dishonored, nothing worth,
> in the dark corner, as you would kennel a vicious dog,
> and burst in an outrush of tears, that came that day
> where smiles would not, and hid the streaming of my grief.
> Hear such, and carve the letters of it on your heart.   450

Chorus

> Let words such as these
> drip deep in your ears, but on a quiet heart.
> So far all stands as it stands;
> what is to come, yourself burn to know.
> You must be hard, give no ground, to win home.   455

Orestes

> I speak to you. Be with those you love, my father.

Electra

> And I, all in my tears, ask with him.

Chorus

> We gather into murmurous revolt. Hear
> us, hear. Come back into the light.
> Be with us against those we hate.   460

Orestes

> Warstrength shall collide with warstrength; right with right.

Electra

> O gods, be just in what you bring to pass.

Chorus

> My flesh crawls as I listen to them pray.
> The day of doom has waited long.
> They call for it. It may come.   465
>
> O pain grown into the race
> and blood-dripping stroke
> and grinding cry of disaster,
> moaning and impossible weight to bear.
> Sickness that fights all remedy.   470
>
> Here in the house there lies
> the cure for this, not to be brought
> from outside, never from others
> but in themselves, through the fierce wreck and bloodshed.
> Here is a song sung to the gods beneath us.   475

Hear then, you blessed ones under the ground,
and answer these prayers with strength on our side,
free gift for your children's conquest.

Orestes

Father, o King who died no kingly death, I ask
the gift of lordship at your hands, to rule your house.   480

Electra

I too, my father, ask of you such grace as this:
to murder Aegisthus with strong hand, and then go free.

Orestes

So shall your memory have the feasts that men honor
in custom. Otherwise when feasts are gay, and portions
burn for the earth, you shall be there, and none give heed.   485

Electra

I too out of my own full dowership shall bring
libations for my bridal from my father's house.
Of all tombs, yours shall be the lordliest in my eyes.

Orestes

O Earth, let my father emerge to watch me fight.

Electra

Persephone, grant still the wonder of success.   490

Orestes

Think of that bath, father, where you were stripped of life.

Electra

Think of the casting net that they contrived for you.

Orestes

They caught you like a beast in toils no bronzesmith made.

Electra

Rather, hid you in shrouds that were thought out in shame.

Orestes

Will you not waken, father, to these challenges?   495

Electra

> Will you not rear upright that best beloved head?

Orestes

> Send out your right to battle on the side of those
> you love, or give us holds like those they caught you in.
> For they threw you. Would you not see them thrown in turn?

Electra

> Hear one more cry, father, from me. It is my last.   500
> Your nestlings huddle suppliant at your tomb: look forth
> and pity them, female with the male strain alike.
> Do not wipe out this seed of the Pelopidae.
> So, though you died, you shall not yet be dead, for when
> a man dies, children are the voice of his salvation   505
> afterward. Like corks upon the net, these hold
> the drenched and flaxen meshes, and they will not drown.
> Hear us, then. Our complaints are for your sake, and if
> you honor this our argument, you save yourself.

Chorus

> None can find fault with the length of this discourse you drew   510
> out, to show honor to a grave and fate unwept
> before. The rest is action. Since your heart is set
> that way, now you must strike and prove your destiny.

Orestes

> So. But I am not wandering from my strict course
> when I ask why she sent these libations, for what cause   515
> she acknowledges, too late, a crime for which there is
> no cure. Here was a wretched grace brought to a man
> dead and unfeeling. This I fail to understand.
> The offerings are too small for the act done. Pour out
> all your possessions to atone one act of blood,   520
> you waste your work, it is all useless, reason says.
> Explain me this, for I would learn it, if you know.

Chorus

    I know, child, I was there. It was the dreams she had.
    The godless woman had been shaken in the night
    by floating terrors, when she sent these offerings.   525

Orestes

    Do you know the dream, too? Can you tell it to me right?

Chorus

    She told me herself. She dreamed she gave birth to a snake.

Orestes

    What is the end of the story then? What is the point?

Chorus

    She laid it swathed for sleep as if it were a child.

Orestes

    A little monster. Did it want some kind of food?   530

Chorus

    She herself, in the dream, gave it her breast to suck.

Orestes

    How was her nipple not torn by such a beastly thing?

Chorus

    It was. The creature drew in blood along with the milk.

Orestes

    No void dream this. It is the vision of a man.

Chorus

    She woke screaming out of her sleep, shaky with fear,   535
    as torches kindled all about the house, out of
    the blind dark that had been on them, to comfort the queen.
    So now she sends these mourning offerings to be poured
    and hopes they are medicinal for her disease.

Orestes

    But I pray to the earth and to my father's grave   540
    that this dream is for me and that I will succeed.

See, I divine it, and it coheres all in one piece.
If this snake came out of the same place whence I came,
if she wrapped it in robes, as she wrapped me, and if
its jaws gaped wide around the breast that suckled me, 545
and if it stained the intimate milk with an outburst
of blood, so that for fright and pain she cried aloud,
it follows then, that as she nursed this hideous thing
of prophecy, she must be cruelly murdered. I
turn snake to kill her. This is what the dream portends. 550

Chorus

I choose you my interpreter to read these dreams.
So may it happen. Now you must rehearse your side
in their parts. For some, this means the parts they must not play.

Orestes

Simple to tell them. My sister here must go inside.
I charge her to keep secret what we have agreed, 555
so that, as they by treachery killed a man of high
degree, by treachery tangled in the self same net
they too shall die, in the way Loxias has ordained,
my lord Apollo, whose word was never false before.
Disguised as an outlander, for which I have all gear, 560
I shall go to the outer gates with Pylades
whom you see here. He is hereditary friend
and companion-in-arms of my house. We two shall both assume
the Parnassian dialect and imitate the way
they talk in Phocis. If none at the door will take us in 565
kindly, because the house is in a curse of ills,
we shall stay there, till anybody who goes by
the house will wonder why we are shut out, and say:
"why does Aegisthus keep the suppliant turned away
from his gates, if he is hereabouts and knows of this?" 570
But if I once cross the doorstone of the outer gates
and find my man seated upon my father's throne,
or if he comes down to confront me, and uplifts
his eyes to mine, then lets them drop again, be sure,

before he can say: "where does the stranger come from?" I   575
shall plunge my sword with lightning speed, and drop him dead.
Our Fury who is never starved for blood shall drink
for the third time a cupful of unwatered blood.

Electra, keep a careful eye on all within
the house, so that our plans will hold together. You,   580
women: I charge you, hold your tongues religiously.
Be silent if you must, or speak in the way that will
help us. And now I call upon the god who stands
close, to look on, and guide the actions of my sword.

(*Exeunt Orestes and Pylades. Exit separately, Electra.*)

Chorus

Numberless, the earth breeds   585
dangers, and the sober thought of fear.
The bending sea's arms swarm
with bitter, savage beasts.
Torches blossom to burn along
the high space between ground and sky.   590
Things fly, and things walk the earth.
Remember too
the storm and wrath of the whirlwind.

But who can recount all
the high daring in the will   595
of man, and in the stubborn hearts of women
the all-adventurous passions
that couple with man's overthrow.
The female force, the desperate
love crams its resisted way   600
on marriage and the dark embrace
of brute beasts, of mortal men.

Let him, who goes not on flimsy wings
of thought, learn from her,
Althaea, Thestius'
daughter: who maimed her child, and hard   605
of heart, in deliberate guile

set fire to the bloody torch, her own son's
agemate, that from the day he emerged
from the mother's womb crying
shared the measure of all his life   610
down to the marked death day.

And in the legends there is one more, a girl
of blood, figure of hate
who, for the enemy's   615
sake killed one near in blood, seduced by the wrought
golden necklace from Crete,
wherewith Minos bribed her. She sundered
from Nisus his immortal hair
as he all unsuspecting   620
breathed in a tranquil sleep. Foul wretch,
Hermes of death has got her now.

Since I recall cruelties from quarrels long
ago, in vain, and married love turned to bitterness
a house would fend far away   625
by curse; the guile, treacheries of the woman's heart
against a lord armored in
power, a lord his enemies revered,
I prize the hearth not inflamed within the house,
the woman's right pushed not into daring.   630

Of all foul things legends tell the Lemnian
outranks, a vile wizard's charm, detestable
so that man names a hideous
crime "Lemnian" in memory of their wickedness.
When once the gods loathe a breed   635
of men they go outcast and forgotten.
No man respects what the gods have turned against.
What of these tales I gather has no meaning?

The sword edges near the lungs.
It stabs deep, bittersharp,   640
and right drives it. For that which had no right

lies not yet stamped into the ground, although
one in sin transgressed Zeus' majesty.   64?

Right's anvil stands staunch on the ground
and the smith, Destiny, hammers out the sword.
Delayed in glory, pensive from
the murk, Vengeance brings home at last   65c
a child, to wipe out the stain of blood shed long ago.

                                            (Enter Orestes and Pylades.)

Orestes

In there! Inside! Does anyone hear me knocking at
the gate? I will try again. Is anyone at home?
Try a third time. I ask for someone to come from the house,   65?
if Aegisthus lets it welcome friendly visitors.

Servant (inside)

All right, I hear you. Where does the stranger come from, then?

Orestes

Announce me to the masters of the house. It is
to them I come, and I have news for them to hear.
And be quick, for the darkening chariot of night   660
leans to its course; the hour for wayfarers to drop
anchor in some place that entertains all travelers.
Have someone of authority in the house come out,
the lady of the place or, more appropriately,
its lord, for then no delicacy in speaking blurs   665
the spoken word. A man takes courage and speaks out
to another man, and makes clear everything he means.

                                            (Enter Clytaemestra.)

Clytaemestra

Friends, tell me only what you would have, and it is yours.
We have all comforts that go with a house like ours,
hot baths, and beds to charm away your weariness   670
with rest, and the regard of temperate eyes. But if
you have some higher business, more a matter of state,
that is the men's concern, and I will tell them of it.

Orestes

I am a Daulian stranger out of Phocis. As
I traveled with my pack and my own following   675
making for Argos, where my feet are rested now,
I met a man I did not know, nor did he know
me, but he asked what way I took, and told me his.
It was a Phocian, Strophius; for he told me his name
and said: "Friend, since in any case you make for Argos,   680
remember carefully to tell Orestes' parents
that he is dead; please do not let it slip your mind.
Then, if his people decide to have him brought back home,
or bury him where he went to live, all outlander
forever, carry their requests again to me.   685
For as it is the bronze walls of an urn close in
the ashes of a man who has been deeply mourned."

So much I know, no more. But whether I now talk
with those who have authority and concern in this
I do not know. I think his father should be told.   690

Clytaemestra

Ah me. You tell us how we are stormed from head to heel.
Oh curse upon our house, bitter antagonist,
how far your eyes range. What was clean out of your way
your archery brings down with a distant deadly shot
to strip unhappy me of all I ever loved.   695
Even Orestes now! He was so well advised
to keep his foot clear of this swamp of death. But now
set down as traitor the hope that was our healer once
and made us look for a bright revel in our house.

Orestes

I could have wished, with hosts so prosperous as you,   700
to have made myself known by some more gracious news
and so been entertained by you. For what is there
more kindly than the feeling between host and guest?
Yet it had been abuse of duty in my heart

had I not given so great a matter to his friends,   705
being so bound by promise and the stranger's rights.

Clytaemestra

You shall not find that your reception falls below
your worth, nor be any the less our friend for this.
Some other would have brought the news in any case.
But it is the hour for travelers who all day have trudged   710
the long road, to be given the rest that they deserve.
Escort this gentleman with his companion and
his men, to where our masculine friends are made at home.
Look after them, in manner worthy of a house
like ours; you are responsible for their good care.   715
Meanwhile, we shall communicate these matters to
the masters of the house, and with our numerous friends
deliberate the issues of this fatal news.

                                 (*Exeunt all but the Chorus.*)

Chorus

Handmaidens of this house, who help our cause,
how can our lips frame   720
some force that will show for Orestes?
O Lady Earth, Earth Queen, who now
ride mounded over the lord of ships
where the King's corpse lies buried,
hear us, help us.   725
Now the time breaks for Persuasion in stealth
to go down to the pit, with Hermes of death
and the dark, to direct
trial by the sword's fierce edge.

I think our newcomer is at his deadly work;   730
I see Orestes' old nurse coming forth, in tears.

                                        (*Enter Cilissa.*)

Now where away, Cilissa, through the castle gates,
with sorrow as your hireless fellow-wayfarer?

Cilissa

The woman who is our mistress told me to make haste
and summon Aegisthus for the strangers, "so that he 735
can come and hear, as man to man, in more detail
this news that they have brought." She put a sad face on
before the servants, to hide the smile inside her eyes
over this work that has been done so happily
for her—though on this house the curse is now complete 740
from the plain story that the stranger men have brought.
But as for that Aegisthus, oh, he will be pleased
enough to hear the story. Poor unhappy me,
all my long-standing mixture of misfortunes, hard
burden enough, here in this house of Atreus, 745
when it befell me made the heart ache in my breast.
But never yet did I have to bear a hurt like this.
I took the other troubles bravely as they came:
but now, darling Orestes! I wore out my life
for him. I took him from his mother, brought him up. 750
There were times when he screamed at night and woke me from
my rest; I had to do many hard tasks, and now
useless; a baby is like a beast, it does not think
but you have to nurse it, do you not, the way it wants.
For the child still in swaddling clothes can not tell us 755
if he is hungry or thirsty, if he needs to make
water. Children's young insides are a law to themselves.
I needed second sight for this, and many a time
I think I missed, and had to wash the baby's clothes.
The nurse and laundrywoman had a combined duty 760
and that was I. I was skilled in both handicrafts,
and so Orestes' father gave him to my charge.
And now, unhappy, I am told that he is dead
and go to take the story to that man who has
defiled our house; he will be glad to hear such news. 765

Chorus

Did she say he should come back armed in any way?

Cilissa

How, armed? Say it again. I do not understand.

Chorus

Was he to come with bodyguards, or by himself?

Cilissa

She said to bring his followers, the men-at-arms.

Chorus

Now, if you hate our master, do not tell him that,   770
but simply bid him come as quickly as he can
and cheerfully. In that way he will not take fright.
It is the messenger who makes the bent word straight.

Cilissa

But are you happy over what I have told you?

Chorus

Perhaps: if Zeus might turn our evil wind to good.   775

Cilissa

How so? Orestes, once hope of the house, is gone.

Chorus

Not yet. It would be a poor seer who saw it thus.

Cilissa

What is this? Have you some news that has not been told?

Chorus

Go on and take your message, do as you were bid.
The gods' concerns are what concern only the gods.   780

Cilissa

I will go then and do all this as you have told
me to. May all be for the best. So grant us god.

(*Exit Cilissa.*)

Chorus

Now to my supplication, Zeus,
father of Olympian gods,

grant that those who struggle hard to see   785
temperate things done in the house win their aim
in full. All that I spoke
was spoken in right. Yours, Zeus, to protect.

Zeus, Zeus, make him who is now
in the house stand above those who   790
hate. If you rear him to greatness,
double and three times
and blithely he will repay you.

See the colt of this man whom you loved
harnessed to the chariot   795
of suffering. Set upon the race he runs
sure control. Make us not see him break
stride, but clean down the course
hold the strain of his striding speed.

You that, deep in the house   800
sway their secret pride of wealth,
hear us, gods of sympathy.
For things done in time past
wash out the blood in fair-spoken verdict.
Let the old murder in   805
the house breed no more.

And you, who keep, magnificent, the hallowed and huge
cavern, o grant that the man's house lift up its head
and look on the shining of daylight
and liberty with eyes made
glad with gazing out from the helm of darkness.   810

And with right may the son
of Maia lend his hand, strong to send
wind fair for action, if he will.
Much else lies secret he may show at need.   815
He speaks the markless word, by
night hoods darkness on the eyes
nor shows more plainly when the day is there.

Then at last we shall sing
for deliverance of the house   820
the woman's song that sets the wind
fair, no thin drawn and grief
struck wail, but this: "The ship sails fair."
My way, mine, the advantage piles here, with wreck
and ruin far from those I love.   825

Be not fear struck when your turn comes in the action
but with a great cry *Father*
when she cries *Child* to you
go on through with the innocent murder.   830

Yours to raise high within
your body the heart of Perseus
and for those under the ground you loved
and those yet above, exact
what their bitter passion may desire; make   835
disaster a thing of blood inside the house;
wipe out the man stained with murder.

                                            (*Enter Aegisthus.*)

Aegisthus

It is not without summons that I come, but called
by messenger, with news that there are strangers here
arrived, telling a story that brings no delight: 840
the death of Orestes. For our house, already bitten
and poisoned, to take this new load upon itself
would be a thing of dripping fear and blood. Yet how
shall I pass upon these rumors? As the living truth?
For messages made out of women's terror leap   845
high in the upward air and empty die. Do *you*
know anything of this by which to clear my mind?

Chorus

We heard, yes. But go on inside and hear it from
the strangers. Messengers are never quite so sure
as a man's questions answered by the men themselves.   850

Aegisthus

I wish to question, carefully, this messenger
and learn if he himself was by when the man died
or if he heard but some blind rumor and so speaks.
The mind has eyes, not to be easily deceived.

(Exit Aegisthus.)

Chorus

Zeus, Zeus, what shall I say, where make   855
a beginning of prayer for the gods' aid?
My will is good
but how shall I speak to match my need?
The bloody edges of the knives that rip
man-flesh are moving to work. It will mean   860
utter and final ruin imposed
on Agamemnon's
house: or our man will kindle a flame
and light of liberty, win the domain
and huge treasure again of his fathers.   865
Forlorn challenger, though blessed by god,
Orestes must come to grips with two,
so wrestle. Yet may he throw them.

(A cry is heard from inside the house.)

Listen, it goes   870
but how? What has been done in the house?
Stand we aside until the work is done, for so
we shall not seem to be accountable in this
foul business. For the fight is done, the issue drawn.

(Enter a follower of Aegisthus.)

Follower

O sorrow, all is sorrow for our stricken lord.   875
Raise up again a triple cry of sorrow, for
Aegisthus lives no longer. Open there, open
quick as you may, and slide back the doorbars on the women's
gates. It will take the strength of a young arm, but not
to fight for one who is dead and done for. What use there? 880

Ahoy!
My cry is to the deaf and I babble in vain
at sleepers to no purpose. Clytaemestra, where
is she, does what? Her neck is on the razor's edge
and ripe for lopping, as she did to others before.

(Enter Clytaemestra.)

Clytaemestra

What is this, and why are you shouting in the house?   885

Follower

I tell you, he is alive and killing the dead.

Clytaemestra

Ah, so. You speak in riddles, but I read the rhyme.
We have been won with the treachery by which we slew.
Bring me quick, somebody, an ax to kill a man

(Exit follower.)

and we shall see if we can beat him before we   890
go down—so far gone are we in this wretched fight.

(Enter Orestes and Pylades with swords drawn.)

Orestes

You next: the other one in there has had enough.

Clytaemestra

Beloved, strong Aegisthus, are you dead indeed?

Orestes

You love your man, then? You shall lie in the same grave
with him, and never be unfaithful even in death.   895

Clytaemestra

Hold, my son. Oh take pity, child, before this breast
where many a time, a drowsing baby, you would feed
and with soft gums sucked in the milk that made you strong.

Orestes

What shall I do, Pylades? Be shamed to kill my mother?

Pylades

    What then becomes thereafter of the oracles   900
    declared by Loxias at Pytho? What of sworn oaths?
    Count all men hateful to you rather than the gods.

Orestes

    I judge that you win. Your advice is good.

                             (*To Clytaemestra.*)
                    Come here.
    My purpose is to kill you over his body.
    You thought him bigger than my father while he lived.   905
    Die then and sleep beside him, since he is the man
    you love, and he you should have loved got only your hate.

Clytaemestra

    I raised you when you were little. May I grow old with you?

Orestes

    You killed my father. Would you make your home with me?

Clytaemestra

    Destiny had some part in that, my child.

Orestes

                           Why then   910
    destiny has so wrought that this shall be your death.

Clytaemestra

    A mother has her curse, child. Are you not afraid?

Orestes

    No. You bore me and threw me away, to a hard life.

Clytaemestra

    I sent you to a friend's house. This was no throwing away.

Orestes

    I was born of a free father. You sold me.   915

Clytaemestra

    So? Where then is the price that I received for you?

Orestes

I could say. It would be indecent to tell you.

Clytaemestra

Or if you do, tell also your father's vanities.

Orestes

Blame him not. He suffered while you were sitting here at home.

Clytaemestra

It hurts women to be kept from their men, my child.   920

Orestes

The man's hard work supports the women who sit at home.

Clytaemestra

I think, child, that you mean to kill your mother.

Orestes

                                        No.

It will be you who kill yourself. It will not be I.

Clytaemestra

Take care. Your mother's curse, like dogs, will drag you down.

Orestes

How shall I escape my father's curse, if I fail here?   925

Clytaemestra

I feel like one who wastes live tears upon a tomb.

Orestes

Yes, this is death, your wages for my father's fate.

Clytaemestra

You are the snake I gave birth to, and gave the breast.

Orestes

Indeed, the terror of your dreams saw things to come
clearly. You killed, and it was wrong. Now suffer wrong.   930

(*Orestes and Pylades take Clytaemestra inside the house.*)

Chorus

I have sorrow even for this pair in their twofold
downfall. But since Orestes had the hardiness
to end this chain of bloodlettings, here lies our choice,
that the eyes' light in this house shall not utterly die.

Justice came at the last to Priam and all his sons   935
and it was heavy and hard,
but into the house of Agamemnon returned
the double lion, the double assault,
and the Pythian-steered exile
drove home to the hilt   940
vengeance, moving strongly in guidance sent by the god.

Raise up the high cry o over our lordships' house
won free of distress, free of its fortunes wasted
by two stained with murder,
free of its mournful luck.   945

He came back; his work lay in the secret attack
and it was stealthy and hard
but in the fighting his hand was steered by the very daughter
of Zeus: Right we call her,
mortals who speak of her and name her well. Her wind   950
is fury and death visited upon those she hates.

All that Loxias, who on Parnassus holds
the huge, the deep cleft in the ground, shrilled aloud,
by guile that is no guile   955
returns now to assault the wrong done and grown old.
Divinity keeps, we know not how, strength to resist
surrender to the wicked.
The power that holds the sky's majesty wins our worship.   960

Light is here to behold.
The big bit that held our house is taken away.
Rise up, you halls, arise; for time grown too long
you lay tumbled along the ground.

Time brings all things to pass. Presently time shall cross   965
the outgates of the house after the stain is driven
entire from the hearth
by ceremonies that wash clean and cast out the furies.
The dice of fortune shall be thrown once more, and lie
in a fair fall smiling   970
up at the new indwellers come to live in the house.

> (*The doors of the house open, to show Orestes standing over the
> bodies of Clytaemestra and Aegisthus. His attendants display
> the robe in which Clytaemestra had entangled Agamem-
> non and which she displayed after his murder.*)

Orestes

Behold the twin tyrannies of our land, these two
who killed my father and who sacked my house. For a time
they sat upon their thrones and kept their pride of state,   975
and they are lovers still. So may you judge by what
befell them, for as they were pledged their oath abides.
They swore together death for my unhappy sire
and swore to die together. Now they keep their oath.

Behold again, o audience of these evil things,   980
the engine against my wretched father they devised,
the hands' entanglement, the hobbles for his feet.
Spread it out. Stand around me in a circle and
display this net that caught a man. So shall, not my
father, but that great father who sees all, the Sun,   985
look on my mother's sacrilegious handiwork
and be a witness for me in my day of trial
how it was in all right that I achieved this death,
my mother's: for of Aegisthus' death I take no count:
he has his seducer's punishment, no more than law.   990

But she, who plotted this foul death against the man
by whom she carried the weight of children underneath
her zone, burden once loved, shown hard and hateful now,
what does she seem to be? Some water snake, some viper

whose touch is rot even to him who felt no fang   995
strike, by that brutal and wrong daring in her heart.

And this thing: what shall I call it and be right, in all
eloquence? Trap for an animal or winding sheet
for dead man? Or bath curtain? Since it is a net,
robe you could call it, to entangle a man's feet.   1000
Some highwayman might own a thing like this, to catch
the wayfarer and rob him of his money and
so make a living. With a treacherous thing like this
he could take many victims and go warm within.

May no such wife as she was come to live with me.   1005
Sooner, let God destroy me, with no children born.

Chorus

Ah, but the pitiful work.
Dismal the death that was your ending.
He is left alive; pain flowers for him.

Orestes

Did she do it or did she not? My witness is   1010
this great robe. It was thus she stained Aegisthus' sword.
Dip it and dip it again, the smear of blood conspires
with time to spoil the beauty of this precious thing.
Now I can praise him, now I can stand by to mourn
and speak before this web that killed my father; yet   1015
I grieve for the thing done, the death, and all our race.
I have won; but my victory is soiled, and has no pride.

Chorus

There is no mortal man who shall turn
unhurt his life's course to an end not marred.
There is trouble here. There is more to come.   1020

Orestes

I would have you know, I see not how this thing will end.
I am a charioteer whose course is wrenched outside
the track, for I am beaten, my rebellious senses

bolt with me headlong and the fear against my heart
is ready for the singing and dance of wrath. But while   1025
I hold some grip still on my wits, I say publicly
to my friends: I killed my mother not without some right.
My father's murder stained her, and the gods' disgust.
As for the spells that charmed me to such daring, I
give you in chief the seer of Pytho, Loxias. He   1030
declared I could do this and not be charged with wrong.
Of my evasion's punishment I will not speak:
no archery could hit such height of agony.
And look upon me now, how I go armored in
leafed branch and garland on my way to the centrestone   1035
and sanctuary, and Apollo's level place,
the shining of the fabulous fire that never dies,
to escape this blood that is my own. Loxias ordained
that I should turn me to no other shrine than this.
To all men of Argos in time to come I say   1040
they shall be witness, how these evil things were done.
I go, an outcast wanderer from this land, and leave
behind, in life, in death, the name of what I did.

Chorus

No, what you did was well done. Do not therefore bind
your mouth to foul speech. Keep no evil on your lips.   1045
You liberated all the Argive city when
you lopped the heads of these two snakes with one clean stroke.

Orestes

No!
Women who serve this house, they come like gorgons, they
wear robes of black, and they are wreathed in a tangle
of snakes. I can no longer stay.   1050

Chorus

Orestes, dearest to your father of all men
what fancies whirl you? Hold, do not give way to fear.

Orestes

These are no fancies of affliction. They are clear,
and real, and here; the bloodhounds of my mother's hate.

Chorus

It is the blood still wet upon your hands, that makes   1055
this shaken turbulence be thrown upon your sense.

Orestes

Ah, Lord Apollo, how they grow and multiply,
repulsive for the blood drops of their dripping eyes.

Chorus

There is one way to make you clean: let Loxias
touch you, and set you free from these disturbances.   1060

Orestes

You can not see them, but I see them. I am driven
from this place. I can stay here no longer.

(Exit.)

Chorus

Good luck go with you then, and may the god look on
you with favor and guard you in kind circumstance.

Here on this house of the kings the third   1065
storm has broken, with wind
from the inward race, and gone its course.
The children were eaten: there was the first
affliction, the curse of Thyestes.
Next came the royal death, when a man   1070
and lord of Achaean armies went down
killed in the bath. Third
is for the savior. He came. Shall I call
it that, or death? Where
is the end? Where shall the fury of fate   1075
be stilled to sleep, be done with?

(Exeunt.)

THE EUMENIDES

CHARACTERS

Priestess of Apollo, the Pythia

Apollo

Hermes (silent)

Ghost of Clytaemestra

Orestes

Athene

Chorus of Eumenides (Furies)

Second Chorus; women of Athens

Jurymen, herald, citizens of Athens (all silent parts)

THE EUMENIDES

SCENE: *For the first part of the play [1–234] the scene is Delphi, before the sanctuary of Pythian Apollo. The action of the rest of the play (235 to the end) takes place at Athens, on the Acropolis before the temple of Athene. A simple change in the backdrop will indicate the shift.*

(*Enter, alone, the Pythia.*)

Pythia

I give first place of honor in my prayer to her
who of the gods first prophesied, the Earth; and next
to Themis, who succeeded to her mother's place
of prophecy; so runs the legend; and in third
succession, given by free consent, not won by force,   5
another Titan daughter of Earth was seated here.
This was Phoebe. She gave it as a birthday gift
to Phoebus, who is called still after Phoebe's name.
And he, leaving the pond of Delos and the reef,
grounded his ship at the roadstead of Pallas, then   10
made his way to this land and a Parnassian home.
Deep in respect for his degree Hephaestus' sons
conveyed him here, for these are builders of roads, and changed
the wilderness to a land that was no wilderness.
He came so, and the people highly honored him,   15
with Delphus, lord and helmsman of the country. Zeus
made his mind full with godship and prophetic craft
and placed him, fourth in a line of seers, upon this throne.
So, Loxias is the spokesman of his father, Zeus.
These are the gods I set in the proem of my prayer.   20
But Pallas-before-the-temple has her right in all
I say. I worship the nymphs where the Corycian rock
is hollowed inward, haunt of birds and paced by gods.
Bromius, whom I forget not, sways this place. From here
in divine form he led his Bacchanals in arms   25

to hunt down Pentheus like a hare in the deathtrap.
I call upon the springs of Pleistus, on the power
of Poseidon, and on final loftiest Zeus,
then go to sit in prophecy on the throne. May all
grant me that this of all my entrances shall be   30
the best by far. If there are any Hellenes here
let them draw lots, so enter, as the custom is.
My prophecy is only as the god may guide.

(*She enters the temple and almost immediately comes out again.*)

Things terrible to tell and for the eyes to see
terrible drove me out again from Loxias' house   35
so that I have no strength and cannot stand on springing
feet, but run with hands' help and my legs have no speed.
An old woman afraid is nothing: a child, no more.
    See, I am on my way to the wreath-hung recess
and on the centrestone I see a man with god's   40
defilement on him postured in the suppliant's seat
with blood dripping from his hands and from a new-drawn
    sword,
holding too a branch that had grown high on an olive
tree, decorously wrapped in a great tuft of wool,
and the fleece shone. So far, at least, I can speak clear.   45
    In front of this man slept a startling company
of women lying all upon the chairs. Or not
women, I think I call them rather gorgons, only
not gorgons either, since their shape is not the same.
I saw some creatures painted in a picture once,   50
who tore the food from Phineus, only these had no
wings, that could be seen; they are black and utterly
repulsive, and they snore with breath that drives one back.
From their eyes drips the foul ooze, and their dress is such
as is not right to wear in the presence of the gods'   55
statues, nor even into any human house.
I have never seen the tribe that owns this company
nor know what piece of earth can claim with pride it bore

such brood, and without hurt and tears for labor given.
　　Now after this the master of the house must take　　　　60
his own measures: Apollo Loxias, who is very strong
and heals by divination; reads portentous signs,
and so clears out the houses others hold as well.

(Exit. The doors of the temple open and show Orestes sur-
rounded by the sleeping Furies, Apollo and
Hermes beside him.)

Apollo

I will not give you up. Through to the end standing
your guardian, whether by your side or far away,　　　　65
I shall not weaken toward your enemies. See now
how I have caught and overpowered these lewd creatures.
The repulsive maidens have been stilled to sleep, those gray
and aged children, they with whom no mortal man,
no god, nor even any beast, will have to do.　　　　70
It was because of evil they were born, because
they hold the evil darkness of the Pit below
Earth, loathed alike by men and by the heavenly gods.
Nevertheless, run from them, never weaken. They
will track you down as you stride on across the long　　　　75
land, and your driven feet forever pound the earth,
on across the main water and the circle-washed
cities. Be herdsman to this hard march. Never fail
until you come at last to Pallas' citadel.
Kneel there, and clasp the ancient idol in your arms,　　　　80
and there we shall find those who will judge this case, and words
to say that will have magic in their figures. Thus
you will be rid of your afflictions, once for all.
For it was I who made you strike your mother down.

Orestes

My lord Apollo, you understand what it means to do　　　　85
no wrong. Learn also what it is not to neglect.
None can mistrust your power to do good, if you will.

Apollo

Remember: the fear must not give you a beaten heart.
Hermes, you are my brother from a single sire.
Look after him, and as you are named the god who guides,   90
be such in strong fact. He is my suppliant. Shepherd him
with fortunate escort on his journeys among men.
The wanderer has rights which Zeus acknowledges.

(*Exit Apollo, then Orestes guided by Hermes. Enter the
ghost of Clytaemestra.*)

Clytaemestra

You would sleep, then? And what use are you, if you sleep?
It is because of you I go dishonored thus   95
among the rest of the dead. Because of those I killed
my bad name among the perished suffers no eclipse
but I am driven in disgrace. I say to you
that I am charged with guilt most grave by these. And yet
I suffered too, horribly, and from those most dear,   100
yet none among the powers is angered for my sake
that I was slaughtered, and by matricidal hands.
Look at these gashes in my heart, think where they came
from. Eyes illuminate the sleeping brain,
but in the daylight man's future cannot be seen.   105
  Yet I have given you much to lap up, outpourings
without wine, sober propitiations, sacrificed
in secrecy of night and on a hearth of fire
for you, at an hour given to no other god.
Now I watch all these honors trampled into the ground,   110
and he is out and gone away like any fawn
so lightly, from the very middle of your nets,
sprung clear, and laughing merrily at you. Hear me.
It is my life depends upon this spoken plea.
Think then, o goddesses beneath the ground. For I,   115
the dream of Clytaemestra, call upon your name.

(*The Furies stir in their sleep and whimper.*)

Clytaemestra

Oh, whimper, then, but your man has got away and gone
far. He has friends to help him, who are not like mine.

(*They whimper again.*)   120

Clytaemestra

Too much sleep and no pity for my plight. I stand,
his mother, here, killed by Orestes. He is gone.

(*They moan in their sleep.*)

Clytaemestra

You moan, you sleep. Get on your feet quickly, will you?
What have you yet got done, except to do evil?   125

(*They moan again.*)

Clytaemestra

Sleep and fatigue, two masterful conspirators,
have dimmed the deadly anger of the mother-snake.

(*The Chorus start violently, then speak in their sleep.*)

Chorus

Get him, get him, get him, get him. Make sure.   130

Clytaemestra

The beast you are after is a dream, but like the hound
whose thought of hunting has no lapse, you bay him on.
What are you about? Up, let not work's weariness
beat you, nor slacken with sleep so you forget my pain.
Scold your own heart and hurt it, as it well deserves,   135
for this is discipline's spur upon her own. Let go
upon this man the stormblasts of your bloodshot breath,
wither him in your wind, after him, hunt him down
once more, and shrivel him in your vitals' heat and flame.

(*The ghost disappears, and the Chorus waken and, as they
waken, speak severally.*)

« 139 »

Chorus

Waken. You are awake, wake her, as I did you.   140
You dream still? On your feet and kick your sleep aside.
Let us see whether this morning-song means vanity.

                            (*Here they begin to howl.*)

Sisters, we have had wrong done us.
When I have undergone so much and all in vain.
Suffering, suffering, bitter, oh shame shame,   145
unendurable wrong.
The hunted beast has slipped clean from our nets and gone.
Sleep won me, and I lost my capture.

Shame, son of Zeus! Robber is all you are.
A young god, you have ridden down powers gray with age,   150
taken the suppliant, though a godless man, who hurt
the mother who gave him birth.
Yourself a god, you stole the matricide away.
Where in this act shall any man say there is right?

The accusation came upon me from my dreams,   155
and hit me, as with goad in the mid-grip of his fist
the charioteer strikes,
but deep, beneath lobe and heart.
The executioner's cutting whip is mine to feel   160
and the weight of pain is big, heavy to bear.

Such are the actions of the younger gods. These hold
by unconditional force, beyond all right, a throne
that runs reeking blood,
blood at the feet, blood at the head.   165
The very stone centre of earth here in our eyes horrible
with blood and curse stands plain to see.

Himself divine, he has spoiled his secret shrine's
hearth with the stain, driven and hallooed the action on.   170
He made man's way cross the place of the ways of god
and blighted age-old distributions of power.

He has wounded me, but he shall not get this man away.
Let him hide under the ground, he shall never go free.   175
Cursed suppliant, he shall feel against his head
another murderer rising out of the same seed.

(*Apollo enters again from his sanctuary.*)

Apollo

Get out, I tell you, go and leave this house. Away
in haste, from your presence set the mantic chamber free,   180
else you may feel the flash and bite of a flying snake
launched from the twisted thong of gold that spans my bow
to make you in your pain spew out the black and foaming
blood of men, vomit the clots sucked from their veins.
This house is no right place for such as you to cling   185
upon; but where, by judgment given, heads are lopped
and eyes gouged out, throats cut, and by the spoil of sex
the glory of young boys is defeated, where mutilation
lives, and stoning, and the long moan of tortured men
spiked underneath the spine and stuck on pales. Listen   190
to how the gods spit out the manner of that feast
your loves lean to. The whole cast of your shape is guide
to what you are, the like of whom should hole in the cave
of the blood-reeking lion, not in oracular
interiors, like mine nearby, wipe off your filth.   195
Out then, you flock of goats without a herdsman, since
no god has such affection as to tend this brood.

Chorus

My lord Apollo, it is your turn to listen now.
Your own part in this is more than accessory.
You are the one who did it; all the guilt is yours.   200

Apollo

So? How? Continue speaking, until I understand.

Chorus

You gave this outlander the word to kill his mother.

Apollo

The word to exact price for his father. What of that?

Chorus

You then dared take him in, fresh from his bloodletting.

Apollo

Yes, and I told him to take refuge in this house.   205

Chorus

You are abusive then to those who sped him here?

Apollo

Yes. It was not for you to come near this house;

Chorus

                       and yet
we have our duty. It was to do what we have done.

Apollo

An office? You? Sound forth your glorious privilege.

Chorus

This: to drive matricides out of their houses.   210

Apollo

                           Then
what if it be the woman and she kills her man?

Chorus

Such murder would not be the shedding of kindred blood.

Apollo

You have made into a thing of no account, no place,
the sworn faith of Zeus and of Hera, lady
of consummations, and Cypris by such argument   215
is thrown away, outlawed, and yet the sweetest things
in man's life come from her, for married love between
man and woman is bigger than oaths, guarded by right
of nature. If when such kill each other you relent
so as not to take vengeance nor eye them in wrath,   220

« 142 »

then I deny your manhunt of Orestes goes
with right. I see that one cause moves you to strong rage
but on the other clearly you are unmoved to act.
Pallas divine shall review the pleadings of this case.

Chorus

Nothing will ever make me let that man go free. 225

Apollo

Keep after him then, and make more trouble for yourselves.

Chorus

Do not try to dock my privilege by argument.

Apollo

I would not take your privilege if you gave it me.

Chorus

No, for you are called great beside the throne of Zeus
already, but the motherblood drives me, and I go 230
to win my right upon this man and hunt him down.

Apollo

But I shall give the suppliant help and rescue, for
if I willingly fail him who turns to me for aid,
his wrath, before gods and men, is a fearful thing.

> (*They go out, separately. The scene is now Athens, on the
> Acropolis before the temple and statue of Athene.
> Orestes enters and takes suppliant posture
> at the feet of the statue.*)

Orestes

My lady Athene, it is at Loxias' behest 235
I come. Then take in of your grace the wanderer
who comes, no suppliant, not unwashed of hand, but one
blunted at last, and worn and battered on the outland
habitations and the beaten ways of men.
Crossing the dry land and the sea alike, keeping 240
the ordinances of Apollo's oracle

I come, goddess, before your statue and your house
to keep watch here and wait the issue of my trial.

(*The Chorus enter severally, looking for Orestes.*)

Chorus

So. Here the man has left a clear trail behind; keep on,   245
keep on, as the unspeaking accuser tells us, by
whose sense, like hounds after a bleeding fawn, we trail
our quarry by the splash and drip of blood. And now
my lungs are blown with abundant and with wearisome
work, mankilling. My range has been the entire extent
of land, and, flown unwinged across the open water,   250
I am here, and give way to no ship in my pursuit.
Our man has gone to cover somewhere in this place.
The welcome smell of human blood has told me so.

Look again, look again,
search everywhere, let   255
not the matricide
steal away and escape.

(*They see Orestes.*)

See there! He clings to defence
again, his arms winding the immortal goddess'
image, so tries to be quit out of our hands.   260
It shall not be. His mother's blood spilled on the ground
can not come back again.
It is all soaked and drained into the ground and gone.

You must give back for her blood from the living man
red blood of your body to suck, and from your own   265
I could feed, with bitter-swallowed drench,
turn your strength limp while yet you live and drag you down
where you must pay for the pain of the murdered mother,
and watch the rest of the mortals stained with violence
against god or guest   270
or hurt parents who were close and dear,
each with the pain upon him that his crime deserves.
Hades is great, Hades calls men to reckoning

there under the ground,
sees all, and cuts it deep in his recording mind.   275

Orestes

I have been beaten and been taught, I understand
the many rules of absolution, where it is right
to speak and where be silent. In this action now
speech has been ordered by my teacher, who is wise.
The stain of blood dulls now and fades upon my hand.   280
My blot of matricide is being washed away.
When it was fresh still, at the hearth of the god, Phoebus,
this was absolved and driven out by sacrifice
of swine, and the list were long if I went back to tell
of all I met who were not hurt by being with me.   285
Time in his aging overtakes all things alike.
Now it is from pure mouth and with good auspices
I call upon Athene, queen of this land, to come
and rescue me. She, without work of her spear, shall win
myself and all my land and all the Argive host   290
to stand her staunch companion for the rest of time.
Whether now ranging somewhere in the Libyan land
beside her father's crossing and by Triton's run
of waters she sets upright or enshrouded foot
rescuing there her friends, or on the Phlegraean flat   295
like some bold man of armies sweeps with eyes the scene,
let her come! She is a god and hears me far away.
So may she set me free from what is at my back.

Chorus

Neither Apollo nor Athene's strength must win
you free, save you from going down forgotten, without   300
knowing where joy lies anywhere inside your heart,
blood drained, chewed dry by the powers of death, a wraith, a
   shell.
You will not speak to answer, spew my challenge away?
You are consecrate to me and fattened for my feast,

and you shall feed me while you live, not cut down first 305
at the altar. Hear the spell I sing to bind you in.

Come then, link we our choral. Ours
to show forth the power
and terror of our music, declare
our rights of office, how we conspire 310
to steer men's lives.
We hold we are straight and just. If a man
can spread his hands and show they are clean,
no wrath of ours shall lurk for him.
Unscathed he walks through his life time. 315
But one like this man before us, with stained
hidden hands, and the guilt upon him,
shall find us beside him, as witnesses
of the truth, and we show clear in the end
to avenge the blood of the murdered. 320

Mother, o my mother night, who gave me
birth, to be a vengeance on the seeing
and the blind, hear me. For Leto's
youngling takes my right away,
stealing from my clutch the prey 325
that crouches, whose blood would wipe
at last the motherblood away.

Over the beast doomed to the fire
this is the chant, scatter of wits,
frenzy and fear, hurting the heart, 330
song of the Furies
binding brain and blighting blood
in its stringless melody.

This the purpose that the all-involving
destiny spun, to be ours and to be shaken 335
never: when mortals assume outrage
of own hand in violence,
these we dog, till one goes

under earth. Nor does death
set them altogether free.   340

Over the beast doomed to the fire
this is the chant, scatter of wits,
frenzy and fear, hurting the heart,
song of the Furies
binding brain and blighting blood   345
in its stringless melody.

When we were born such lots were assigned for our keeping.
So the immortals must hold hands off, nor is there   350
one who shall sit at our feasting.
For sheer white robes I have no right and no portion.

I have chosen overthrow
of houses, where the Battlegod   355
grown within strikes near and dear
down. So we swoop upon this man
here. He is strong, but we wear him down
for the blood that is still wet on him.

Here we stand in our haste to wrench from all others   360
these devisings, make the gods clear of our counsels
so that even appeal comes
not to them, since Zeus has ruled our blood dripping company   365
outcast, nor will deal with us.

I have chosen overthrow
of houses, where the Battlegod
grown within strikes near and dear
down. So we swoop upon this man
here. He is strong, but we wear him down
for the blood that is still wet on him.

Men's illusions in their pride under the sky melt
down, and are diminished into the ground, gone
before the onset of our black robes, pulsing   370
of our vindictive feet against them.

For with a long leap from high
above and dead drop of weight
I bring foot's force crashing down
to cut the legs from under even   375
the runner, and spill him to ruin.

He falls, and does not know in the daze of his folly.
Such in the dark of man is the mist of infection
that hovers, and moaning rumor tells how his house lies
under fog that glooms above.   380

For with a long leap from high
above, and dead drop of weight,
I bring foot's force crashing down
to cut the legs from under even
the runner, and spill him to ruin.

All holds. For we are strong and skilled;
we have authority; we hold
memory of evil; we are stern
nor can men's pleadings bend us. We
drive through our duties, spurned, outcast   385
from gods, driven apart to stand in light
not of the sun. So sheer with rock are ways
for those who see, as upon those whose eyes are lost.

Is there a man who does not fear
this, does not shrink to hear   390
how my place has been ordained,
granted and given by destiny
and god, absolute? Privilege
primeval yet is mine, nor am I without place
though it be underneath the ground   395
and in no sunlight and in gloom that I must stand.

(Athene enters, in full armor.)

Athene

From far away I heard the outcry of your call.
It was beside Scamandrus. I was taking seisin
of land, for there the Achaean lords of war and first

fighters gave me large portion of all their spears 400
had won, the land root and stock to be mine for all
eternity, for the sons of Theseus a choice gift.
From there, sped on my weariless feet, I came, wingless
but in the rush and speed of the aegis fold. And now
I see upon this land a novel company 405
which, though it brings no terror to my eyes, brings still
wonder. Who are you? I address you all alike,
both you, the stranger kneeling at my image here,
and you, who are like no seed ever begotten, not 410
seen ever by the gods as goddesses, nor yet
stamped in the likenesses of any human form.
But no. This is the place of the just. Its rights forbid
even the innocent to speak evil of his mates.

Chorus
Daughter of Zeus, you shall hear all compressed to brief 415
measure. We are the gloomy children of the night.
Curses they call us in our homes beneath the ground.

Athene
I know your race, then, and the names by which you are called.

Chorus
You shall be told of our position presently.

Athene
I can know that, if one will give me a clear account. 420

Chorus
We drive from home those who have shed the blood of men.

Athene
Where is the place, then, where the killer's flight shall end?

Chorus
A place where happiness is nevermore allowed.

Athene
Is he one? Do you blast him to this kind of flight?

Chorus

Yes. He murdered his mother by deliberate choice. 425

Athene

By random force, or was it fear of someone's wrath?

Chorus

Where is the spur to justify man's matricide?

Athene

Here are two sides, and only half the argument.

Chorus

He is unwilling to give or to accept an oath.

Athene

You wish to be called righteous rather than act right. 430

Chorus

No. How so? Out of the riches of your wit, explain.

Athene

I say, wrong must not win by technicalities.

Chorus

Examine him then yourself. Decide it, and be fair.

Athene

You would turn over authority in this case to me?

Chorus

By all means. Your father's degree, and yours, deserve as much. 435

Athene

Your turn, stranger. What will you say in answer? Speak,
tell me your country and your birth, what has befallen
you, then defend yourself against the anger of these;
if it was confidence in the right that made you sit
to keep this image near my hearth, a supplicant 440
in the tradition of Ixion, sacrosanct.
Give me an answer which is plain to understand.

Orestes

Lady Athene, first I will take the difficult thought
away that lies in these last words you spoke. I am
no supplicant, nor was it because I had a stain   445
upon my hand that I sat at your image. I
will give you a strong proof that what I say is true.
It is the law that the man of the bloody hand must speak
no word until, by action of one who can cleanse,
blood from a young victim has washed his blood away.   450
Long since, at the homes of others, I have been absolved
thus, both by running waters and by victims slain.

I count this scruple now out of the way. Learn next
with no delay where I am from. I am of Argos
and it is to my honor that you ask the name   455
of my father, Agamemnon, lord of seafarers,
and your companion when you made the Trojan city
of Ilium no city any more. He died
without honor when he came home. It was my mother
of the dark heart, who entangled him in subtle gyves   460
and cut him down. The bath is witness to his death.
I was an exile in the time before this. I came back
and killed the woman who gave me birth. I plead guilty.
My father was dear, and this was vengeance for his blood.
Apollo shares responsibility for this.   465
He counterspurred my heart and told me of pains to come
if I should fail to act against the guilty ones.
This is my case. Decide if it be right or wrong.
I am in your hands. Where my fate falls, I shall accept.

Athene

The matter is too big for any mortal man   470
who thinks he can judge it. Even I have not the right
to analyse cases of murder where wrath's edge
is sharp, and all the more since you have come, and clung
a clean and innocent supplicant, against my doors.
You bring no harm to my city. I respect your rights.   475

Yet these, too, have their work. We cannot brush them aside,
and if this action so runs that they fail to win,
the venom of their resolution will return
to infect the soil, and sicken all my land to death.
Here is dilemma. Whether I let them stay or drive   480
them off, it is a hard course and will hurt. Then, since
the burden of the case is here, and rests on me,
I shall select judges of manslaughter, and swear
them in, establish a court into all time to come.

Litigants, call your witnesses, have ready your proofs   485
as evidence under bond to keep this case secure.
I will pick the finest of my citizens, and come
back. They shall swear to make no judgment that is not
just, and make clear where in this action the truth lies.

                                                        (*Exit.*)

Chorus

Here is overthrow of all   490
the young laws, if the claim
of this matricide shall stand
good, his crime be sustained.
Should this be, every man will find a way
to act at his own caprice;   495
over and over again in time
to come, parents shall await
the deathstroke at their children's hands.

We are the Angry Ones. But we
shall watch no more over works   500
of men, and so act. We shall
let loose indiscriminate death.
Man shall learn from man's lot, forejudge
the evils of his neighbor's case,
see respite and windfall in storm:
pathetic prophet who consoles   505
with strengthless cures, in vain.

Nevermore let one who feels
the stroke of accident, uplift
his voice and make outcry, thus: 510
"Oh Justice!
Throned powers of the Furies, help!"
Such might be the pitiful cry
of some father, of the stricken
mother, their appeal. Now   515
the House of Justice has collapsed.

There are times when fear is good.
It must keep its watchful place
at the heart's controls. There is
advantage   520
in the wisdom won from pain.
Should the city, should the man
rear a heart that nowhere goes
in fear, how shall such a one
any more respect the right?   525

Refuse the life of anarchy;
refuse the life devoted to
one master.
The in-between has the power
by God's grant always, though   530
his ordinances vary.
I will speak in defence
of reason: for the very child
of vanity is violence;
but out of health   535
in the heart issues the beloved
and the longed-for, prosperity.

All for all I say to you:
bow before the altar of right.
You shall not   540
eye advantage, and heel
it over with foot of force.

Vengeance will be upon you.
The all is bigger than you.
Let man see this and take   545
care, to mother and father,
and to the guest
in the gates welcomed, give all rights
that befall their position.

The man who does right, free-willed, without constraint   550
shall not lose happiness
nor be wiped out with all his generation.
But the transgressor, I tell you, the bold man
who brings in confusion of goods unrightly won,
at long last and perforce, when ship toils   555
under tempest must strike his sail
in the wreck of his rigging.

He calls on those who hear not, caught inside
the hard wrestle of water.
The spirit laughs at the hot hearted man,   560
the man who said "never to me," watches him
pinned in distress, unable to run free of the crests.
He had good luck in his life. Now
he smashes it on the reef of Right
and drowns, unwept and forgotten.   565

*(Athene re-enters, guiding twelve citizens chosen as jurors
and attended by a herald. Other citizens follow.)*

Athene

Herald, make proclamation and hold in the host
assembled. Let the stabbing voice of the Etruscan
trumpet, blown to the full with mortal wind, crash out
its high call to all the assembled populace
For in the filling of this senatorial ground   570
it is best for all the city to be silent and learn
the measures I have laid down into the rest of time.
So too these litigants, that their case be fairly tried.

(Trumpet call. All take their places. Enter Apollo.)

Chorus

My lord Apollo, rule within your own domain.
What in this matter has to do with you? Declare.   575

Apollo

I come to testify. This man, by observed law,
came to me as suppliant, took his place by hearth and hall,
and it was I who cleaned him of the stain of blood.
I have also come to help him win his case. I bear
responsibility for his mother's murder.

                                                (To Athene.)

                                        You   580
who know the rules, initiate the trial. Preside.

Athene (to the Furies)

I declare the trial opened. Yours is the first word.
For it must justly be the pursuer who speaks first
and opens the case, and makes plain what the action is.

Chorus

We are many, but we shall cut it short. You, then,   585
word against word answer our charges one by one.
Say first, did you kill your mother or did you not?

Orestes

Yes, I killed her. There shall be no denial of that.

Chorus

There are three falls in the match and one has gone to us.

Orestes

So you say. But you have not even thrown your man.   590

Chorus

So. Then how did you kill her? You are bound to say.

Orestes

I do. With drawn sword in my hand I cut her throat.

Chorus

By whose persuasion and advice did you do this?

Orestes

By order of this god, here. So he testifies.

Chorus

The Prophet guided you into this matricide?   595

Orestes

Yes. I have never complained of this. I do not now.

Chorus

When sentence seizes you, you will talk a different way.

Orestes

I have no fear. My father will aid me from the grave.

Chorus

Kill your mother, then put trust in a corpse! Trust on.

Orestes

Yes. She was dirtied twice over with disgrace.   600

Chorus

Tell me how, and explain it to the judges here.

Orestes

She murdered her husband, and thereby my father too.

Chorus

Of this stain, death has set her free. But you still live.

Orestes

When she lived, why did you not descend and drive her out?

Chorus

The man she killed was not of blood congenital.   605

Orestes

But am I then involved with my mother by blood-bond?

Chorus

Murderer, yes. How else could she have nursed you beneath
her heart? Do you forswear your mother's intimate blood?

Orestes

Yours to bear witness now, Apollo, and expound
the case for me, if I was right to cut her down.   610
I will not deny I did this thing, because I did
do it. But was the bloodshed right or not? Decide
and answer. As you answer, I shall state my case.

Apollo

To you, established by Athene in your power,
I shall speak justly. I am a prophet, I shall not   615
lie. Never, for man, woman, nor city, from my throne
of prophecy have I spoken a word, except
that which Zeus, father of Olympians, might command.
This is justice. Recognize then how great its strength.
I tell you, follow our father's will. For not even   620
the oath that binds you is more strong than Zeus is strong.

Chorus

Then Zeus, as you say, authorized the oracle
to this Orestes, stating he could wreak the death
of his father on his mother, and it would have no force?

Apollo

It is not the same thing for a man of blood to die   625
honored with the king's staff given by the hand of god,
and that by means of a woman, not with the far cast
of fierce arrows, as an Amazon might have done,
but in a way that you shall hear, o Pallas and you
who sit in state to judge this action by your vote.   630

He had come home from his campaigning. He had done
better than worse, in the eyes of a fair judge. She lay
in wait for him. It was the bath. When he was at
its edge, she hooded the robe on him, and in the blind
and complex toils tangled her man, and chopped him down.   635

There is the story of the death of a great man,
solemn in all men's sight, lord of the host of ships.

I have called the woman what she was, so that the people
whose duty it is to try this case may be inflamed.

Chorus

Zeus, by your story, gives first place to the father's death.   640
Yet Zeus himself shackled elder Cronus, his own
father. Is this not contradiction? I testify,
judges, that this is being said in your hearing.

Apollo

You foul animals, from whom the gods turn in disgust,
Zeus could undo shackles, such hurt can be made good,   645
and there is every kind of way to get out. But once
the dust has drained down all a man's blood, once the man
has died, there is no raising of him up again.
This is a thing for which my father never made
curative spells. All other states, without effort   650
of hard breath, he can completely rearrange.

Chorus

See what it means to force acquittal of this man.
He has spilled his mother's blood upon the ground. Shall he
then be at home in Argos in his father's house?
What altars of the community shall he use? Is there   655
a brotherhood's lustration that will let him in?

Apollo

I will tell you, and I will answer correctly. Watch.
The mother is no parent of that which is called
her child, but only nurse of the new-planted seed
that grows. The parent is he who mounts. A stranger she   660
preserves a stranger's seed, if no god interfere.
I will show you proof of what I have explained. There can
be a father without any mother. There she stands,
the living witness, daughter of Olympian Zeus,
she who was never fostered in the dark of the womb   665
yet such a child as no goddess could bring to birth.
In all else, Pallas, as I best may understand,

I shall make great your city and its populace.
So I have brought this man to sit beside the hearth
of your house, to be your true friend for the rest of time,   670
so you shall win him, goddess, to fight by your side,
and among men to come this shall stand a strong bond
that his and your own people's children shall be friends.

Athene

Shall I assume that enough has now been said, and tell
the judges to render what they believe a true verdict?   675

Chorus

Every arrow we had has been shot now. We wait
on their decision, to see how the case has gone.

Athene

So then. How shall I act correctly in your eyes?

Apollo

You have heard what you have heard, and as you cast your votes,
good friends, respect in your hearts the oath that you have sworn.   680

Athene

If it please you, men of Attica, hear my decree
now, on this first case of bloodletting I have judged.
For Aegeus' population, this forevermore
shall be the ground where justices deliberate.
Here is the Hill of Ares, here the Amazons   685
encamped and built their shelters when they came in arms
for spite of Theseus, here they piled their rival towers
to rise, new city, and dare his city long ago,
and slew their beasts for Ares. So this rock is named
from then the Hill of Ares. Here the reverence   690
of citizens, their fear and kindred do-no-wrong
shall hold by day and in the blessing of night alike
all while the people do not muddy their own laws
with foul infusions. But if bright water you stain
with mud, you nevermore will find it fit to drink.   695

No anarchy, no rule of a single master. Thus
I advise my citizens to govern and to grace,
and not to cast fear utterly from your city. What
man who fears nothing at all is ever righteous? Such
be your just terrors, and you may deserve and have   700
salvation for your citadel, your land's defence,
such as is nowhere else found among men, neither
among the Scythians, nor the land that Pelops held.
I establish this tribunal. It shall be untouched
by money-making, grave but quick to wrath, watchful   705
to protect those who sleep, a sentry on the land.

These words I have unreeled are for my citizens,
advice into the future. All must stand upright
now, take each man his ballot in his hand, think on
his oath, and make his judgment. For my word is said.   710

Chorus

I give you counsel by no means to disregard
this company. We can be a weight to crush your land.

Apollo

I speak too. I command you to fear, and not
make void the yield of oracles from Zeus and me.

Chorus

You honor bloody actions where you have no right.   715
The oracles you give shall be no longer clean.

Apollo

My father's purposes are twisted then. For he
was appealed to by Ixion, the first murderer.

Chorus

Talk! But for my part, if I do not win the case,
I shall come back to this land and it will feel my weight.   720

Apollo

Neither among the elder nor the younger gods
have you consideration. I shall win this suit.

Chorus

    Such was your action in the house of Pheres. Then
    you beguiled the Fates to let mortals go free from death.

Apollo

    Is it not right to do well by the man who shows   725
    you worship, and above all when he stands in need?

Chorus

    You won the ancient goddesses over with wine
    and so destroyed the orders of an elder time.

Apollo

    You shall not win the issue of this suit, but shall
    be made to void your poison to no enemy's hurt.   730

Chorus

    Since you, a young god, would ride down my elder age,
    I must stay here and listen to how the trial goes,
    being yet uncertain to loose my anger on the state.

Athene

    It is my task to render final judgment here.
    This is a ballot for Orestes I shall cast.   735
    There is no mother anywhere who gave me birth,
    and, but for marriage, I am always for the male
    with all my heart, and strongly on my father's side.
    So, in a case where the wife has killed her husband, lord
    of the house, her death shall not mean most to me. And if   740
    the other votes are even, then Orestes wins.
    You of the jurymen who have this duty assigned,
    shake out the ballots from the vessels, with all speed.

Orestes

    Phoebus Apollo, what will the decision be?

Chorus

    Darkness of night, our mother, are you here to watch?   745

Orestes

This is the end for me. The noose, or else the light.

Chorus

Here our destruction, or our high duties confirmed.

Apollo

Shake out the votes accurately, Athenian friends.
Be careful as you pick them up. Make no mistake.
In the lapse of judgment great disaster comes. The cast   750
of a single ballot has restored a house entire.

Athene

The man before us has escaped the charge of blood.
The ballots are in equal number for each side.

Orestes

Pallas Athene, you have kept my house alive.
When I had lost the land of my fathers you gave me   755
a place to live. Among the Hellenes they shall say:
"A man of Argos lives again in the estates
of his father, all by grace of Pallas Athene, and
Apollo, and with them the all-ordaining god
the Savior"—who remembers my father's death, who looked   760
upon my mother's advocates, and rescues me.
I shall go home now, but before I go I swear
to this your country and to this your multitude
of people into all the bigness of time to be,
that never man who holds the helm of my state shall come   765
against your country in the ordered strength of spears,
but though I lie then in my grave, I still shall wreak
helpless bad luck and misadventure upon all
who stride across the oath that I have sworn: their ways
disconsolate make, their crossings full of evil   770
augury, so they shall be sorry that they moved.
But while they keep the upright way, and hold in high
regard the city of Pallas, and align their spears
to fight beside her, I shall be their gracious spirit.

And so farewell, you and your city's populace.   775
May you outwrestle and overthrow all those who come
against you, to your safety and your spears' success.

(Exit. Exit also Apollo.)

Chorus

Gods of the younger generation, you have ridden down
the laws of the elder time, torn them out of my hands.
I, disinherited, suffering, heavy with anger   780
shall let loose on the land
the vindictive poison
dripping deadly out of my heart upon the ground;
this from itself shall breed
cancer, the leafless, the barren   785
to strike, for the right, their low lands
and drag its smear of mortal infection on the ground.
What shall I do? Afflicted
I am mocked by these people.
I have borne what can not   790
be borne. Great the sorrows and the dishonor upon
the sad daughters of night.

Athene

Listen to me. I would not have you be so grieved.
For you have not been beaten. This was the result   795
of a fair ballot which was even. You were not
dishonored, but the luminous evidence of Zeus
was there, and he who spoke the oracle was he
who ordered Orestes so to act and not be hurt.
Do not be angry any longer with this land   800
nor bring the bulk of your hatred down on it, do not
render it barren of fruit, nor spill the dripping rain
of death in fierce and jagged lines to eat the seeds.
In complete honesty I promise you a place
of your own, deep hidden under ground that is yours by right   805
where you shall sit on shining chairs beside the hearth
to accept devotions offered by your citizens.

Chorus

> Gods of the younger generation, you have ridden down
> the laws of the elder time, torn them out of my hands.
> I, disinherited, suffering, heavy with anger   810
> shall let loose on the land
> the vindictive poison
> dripping deadly out of my heart upon the ground;
> this from itself shall breed
> cancer, the leafless, the barren   815
> to strike, for the right, their low lands
> and drag its smear of mortal infection on the ground.
> What shall I do? Afflicted
> I am mocked by these people.
> I have borne what can not   820
> be borne. Great the sorrow and the dishonor upon
> the sad daughters of night.

Athene

> No, not dishonored. You are goddesses. Do not
> in too much anger make this place of mortal men   825
> uninhabitable. I have Zeus behind me. Do
> we need to speak of that? I am the only god
> who know the keys to where his thunderbolts are locked.
> We do not need such, do we? Be reasonable
> and do not from a reckless mouth cast on the land   830
> spells that will ruin every thing which might bear fruit.
> No. Put to sleep the bitter strength in the black wave
> and live with me and share my pride of worship. Here
> is a big land, and from it you shall win first fruits
> in offerings for children and the marriage rite   835
> for always. Then you will say my argument was good.

Chorus

> That they could treat me so!
> I, the mind of the past, to be driven under the ground
> out cast, like dirt!
> The wind I breathe is fury and utter hate.   840

Earth, ah, earth
what is this agony that crawls under my ribs?
Night, hear me, o Night,
mother. They have wiped me out   845
and the hard hands of the gods
and their treacheries have taken my old rights away.

Athene

I will bear your angers. You are elder born than I
and in that you are wiser far than I. Yet still
Zeus gave me too intelligence not to be despised.   850
If you go away into some land of foreigners,
I warn you, you will come to love this country. Time
in his forward flood shall ever grow more dignified
for the people of this city. And you, in your place
of eminence beside Erechtheus in his house   855
shall win from female and from male processionals
more than all lands of men beside could ever give.
Only in this place that I haunt do not inflict
your bloody stimulus to twist the inward hearts
of young men, raging in a fury not of wine,   860
nor, as if plucking the heart from fighting cocks,
engraft among my citizens that spirit of war
that turns their battle fury inward on themselves.
No, let our wars range outward hard against the man
who has fallen horribly in love with high renown.   865
No true fighter I call the bird that fights at home.
Such life I offer you, and it is yours to take.
Do good, receive good, and be honored as the good
are honored. Share our country, the beloved of god.

Chorus

That they could treat me so!   870
I, the mind of the past, to be driven under the ground
out cast, like dirt!
The wind I breathe is fury and utter hate.
Earth, ah, earth

what is this agony that crawls under my ribs?   875
Night, hear me, o Night,
mother. They have wiped me out
and the hard hands of the gods
and their treacheries have taken my old rights away.   880

Athene

I will not weary of telling you all the good things
I offer, so that you can never say that you,
an elder god, were driven unfriended from the land
by me in my youth, and by my mortal citizens.
But if you hold Persuasion has her sacred place   885
of worship, in the sweet beguilement of my voice,
then you might stay with us. But if you wish to stay
then it would not be justice to inflict your rage
upon this city, your resentment or bad luck
to armies. Yours the baron's portion in this land   890
if you will, in all justice, with full privilege.

Chorus

Lady Athene, what is this place you say is mine?

Athene

A place free of all grief and pain. Take it for yours.

Chorus

If I do take it, shall I have some definite powers?

Athene

No household shall be prosperous without your will.   895

Chorus

You will do this? You will really let me be so strong?

Athene

So we shall straighten the lives of all who worship us.

Chorus

You guarantee such honor for the rest of time?

Athene

I have no need to promise what I can not do.

Chorus

I think you will have your way with me. My hate is going.   900

Athene

Stay here, then. You will win the hearts of others, too.

Chorus

I will put a spell upon the land. What shall it be?

Athene

Something that has no traffic with evil success.
Let it come out of the ground, out of the sea's water,
and from the high air make the waft of gentle gales   905
wash over the country in full sunlight, and the seed
and stream of the soil's yield and of the grazing beasts
be strong and never fail our people as time goes,
and make the human seed be kept alive. Make more
the issue of those who worship more your ways, for as   910
the gardener works in love, so love I best of all
the unblighted generation of these upright men.
All such is yours for granting. In the speech and show
and pride of battle, I myself shall not endure
this city's eclipse in the estimation of mankind.   915

Chorus

I accept this home at Athene's side.
I shall not forget the cause
of this city, which Zeus all powerful and Ares
rule, stronghold of divinities,
glory of Hellene gods, their guarded altar.   920
So with forecast of good
I speak this prayer for them
that the sun's bright magnificence shall break out wave
on wave of all the happiness   925
life can give, across their land

« 167 »

Athene

Here are my actions. In all good will
toward these citizens I establish in power
spirits who are large, difficult to soften.
To them is given the handling entire 930
of men's lives. That man
who has not felt the weight of their hands
takes the strokes of life, knows not whence, not why,
for crimes wreaked in past generations
drag him before these powers. Loud his voice 935
but the silent doom
hates hard, and breaks him to dust.

Chorus

Let there blow no wind that wrecks the trees.
I pronounce words of grace.
Nor blaze of heat blind the blossoms of grown plants, nor 940
cross the circles of its right
place. Let no barren deadly sickness creep and kill.
Flocks fatten. Earth be kind
to them, with double fold of fruit 945
in time appointed for its yielding. Secret child
of earth, her hidden wealth, bestow
blessing and surprise of gods.

Athene

Strong guard of our city, hear you these
and what they portend? Fury is a high queen 950
of strength even among the immortal gods
and the undergods, and for humankind
their work is accomplished, absolute, clear:
for some, singing; for some, life dimmed
in tears; theirs the disposition. 955

Chorus

Death of manhood cut down
before its prime I forbid:

girls' grace and glory find
men to live life with them.
Grant, you who have the power. 960
And o, steering spirits of law,
goddesses of destiny,
sisters from my mother, hear;
in all houses implicate,
in all time heavy of hand 965
on whom your just arrest befalls,
august among goddesses, bestow.

Athene

It is my glory to hear how these
generosities
are given my land. I admire the eyes 970
of Persuasion, who guided the speech of my mouth
toward these, when they were reluctant and wild.
Zeus, who guides men's speech in councils, was too
strong; and my ambition
for good wins out in the whole issue. 975

Chorus

This my prayer: Civil War
fattening on men's ruin shall
not thunder in our city. Let
not the dry dust that drinks
the black blood of citizens 980
through passion for revenge
and bloodshed for bloodshed
be given our state to prey upon.
Let them render grace for grace.
Let love be their common will; 985
let them hate with single heart.
Much wrong in the world thereby is healed.

Athene

Are they taking thought to discover that road
where speech goes straight?

In the terror upon the faces of these   990
I see great good for our citizens.
While with good will you hold in high honor
these spirits, their will shall be good, as you steer
your city, your land
on an upright course clear through to the end.   995

Chorus

Farewell, farewell. High destiny shall be yours
by right. Farewell, citizens
seated near the throne of Zeus,
beloved by the maiden he loves,
civilized as years go by,   1000
sheltered under Athene's wings,
grand even in her father's sight.

Athene

Goddesses, farewell. Mine to lead, as these
attend us, to where
by the sacred light new chambers are given.   1005
Go then. Sped by majestic sacrifice
from these, plunge beneath the ground. There hold
off what might hurt the land; pour in
the city's advantage, success in the end.
You, children of Cranaus, you who keep   1010
the citadel, guide these guests of the state.
For good things given,
your hearts' desire be for good to return.

Chorus

Farewell and again farewell, words spoken twice over,
all who by this citadel,   1015
mortal men, spirits divine,
hold the city of Pallas, grace
this my guestship in your land.
Life will give you no regrets.   1020

Athene

> Well said. I assent to all the burden of your prayers,
> and by the light of flaring torches now attend
> your passage to the deep and subterranean hold,
> as by us walk those women whose high privilege
> it is to guard my image. Flower of all the land   1025
> of Theseus, let them issue now, grave companies,
> maidens, wives, elder women, in processional.
> In the investiture of purple stained robes
> dignify them, and let the torchlight go before
> so that the kindly company of these within   1030
> our ground may shine in the future of strong men to come.

Chorus (by the women who have been forming for processional)

> Home, home, o high, o aspiring
> Daughters of Night, aged children, in blithe processional.
> Bless them, all here, with silence.   1035

> In the primeval dark of earth-hollows
> held in high veneration with rights sacrificial
> bless them, all people, with silence.

> Gracious be, wish what the land wishes,   1040
> follow, grave goddesses, flushed in the flamesprung
> torchlight gay on your journey.
> Singing all follow our footsteps.

> There shall be peace forever between these people
> of Pallas and their guests. Zeus the all seeing   1045
> met with Destiny to confirm it.
> Singing all follow our footsteps.

> > *(Exeunt omnes, in procession.)*